# RECLAIMING THE POWER OF HOODOO

A BEGINNER'S GUIDE TO AFRICAN AMERICAN FOLK
MAGIC TO CULTIVATE PEACE & ABUNDANCE WITHIN
YOUR LIFE THROUGH ROOTWORK & CONJURE

ALISHA J. BROWN

**Copyright © 2022. All rights reserved.**

The content contained within this book may not be reproduced, duplicated or transmitted without direct written permission from the author or the publisher.

Under no circumstances will any blame or legal responsibility be held against the publisher, or author, for any damages, reparation, or monetary loss due to the information contained within this book, either directly or indirectly.

Legal Notice:

This book is copyright protected. It is only for personal use. You cannot amend, distribute, sell, use, quote or paraphrase any part, or the content within this book, without the consent of the author or publisher.

Disclaimer Notice:

Please note the information contained within this document is for educational and entertainment purposes only. All effort has been executed to present accurate, up-to-date, reliable, complete information. No warranties of any kind are declared or implied. Readers acknowledge that the author is not engaged in the rendering of legal, financial, medical, or professional advice. The content within this book has been derived from various sources. Please consult a licensed professional before attempting any techniques outlined in this book.

By reading this document, the reader agrees that under no circumstances is the author responsible for any losses, direct or indirect, that are incurred as a result of the use of the information contained within this document, including, but not limited to, errors, omissions, or inaccuracies.

# CONTENTS

*Introduction*   7

1. A FAR-FROM-BRIEF HISTORY OF HOODOO   13
   The Origins of Hoodoo   15
   From Voodoo to Hoodoo   22
   The Colors of Hoodoo   23
   The Reclaiming of Hoodoo Culture   24
   Conclusion   25

2. HOODOO BELIEFS   27
   Hoodoo and Christianity   27
   Graveyards   33
   Six Principles of Hoodoo   35
   Conclusion   37

3. THE ESSENTIAL TOOLS OF HOODOO PRACTITIONERS   39
   Altar   39
   Incense   46
   Hoodoo Dolls   47
   Conclusion   55

4. ROOTWORK   57
   Getting Your Herbs   58
   Beginner's Herb Guide   63
   Making a Protective Herb Bundle   72
   Herb Garlands   74
   Quick and Easy Ways to Use Herbs   75
   Herbs to Avoid   91
   Conclusion   96

5. SPELLCASTING — 97
   Preparing to Cast a Spell — 98
   Types of Spells — 104
   Conclusion — 126

6. CANDLES, OILS, AND BONES — 127
   Candles Basics — 127
   Oils — 149
   Bones — 156
   Conclusion — 161

7. MOJO BAGS AND SWEETENING JARS — 163
   What Makes a Mojo Bag — 163
   Basic Mojo Bags — 166
   Major Uses for a Mojo Bag — 168
   Sweetening Jars — 169
   Conclusion — 174

   *Afterword* — 175
   *References* — 179

SPECIAL OFFER FROM ALISHA J. BROWN

GET THIS ADDITIONAL BOOK FOR FREE!

JOIN OUR COMMUNITY TO ENJOY INSIDER ACCESS TO ALL OF OUR CURRENT AND FUTURE BOOKS SIMPLY SCAN THE QR CODE BELOW TO RECEIVE THIS FREE BOOK & TO SIGN UP FOR ACCESS

# INTRODUCTION

From the abject horror of films like *White Zombie* and many other early zombie films, to the supernatural absurdity of the *Chucky* franchise, the average consumer is no stranger to Hoodoo or the idea of Hoodoo that has been popularized by American media. Depictions of Hoodoo are often used to demonize 'foreign' spiritual practices and, in contrast, uplift the values of conservative Christianity in comparison. Compared to white Christians' controlled, holy, pure beliefs and practices, Hoodoo is depicted as dark, savage, dangerous, and, most importantly, ethnic.

Witchcraft is depicted very differently depending on whether the practitioner is black or white. White witches are often depicted playfully as quirky young people in the crystal shop or mysterious but ultimately helpful forces of the supernatural. When black witches are defined, they are antagonistic, duplicitous, often inappropriately sexual, and almost always engaging in something deemed spiritually obscene or unholy like grave robbing and human sacrifice. When they are rarely depicted, black people have little representation in the modern witchcraft scene.

A beginner's search into witchcraft will pull up a lot of Celtic or Greco-Roman practices but very little in the way of uniquely black practices. It's easy to conclude that black people just don't do witchcraft outside of fiction. This couldn't be further from the truth. Hoodoo isn't just a fictional antagonistic force but an actual practice. But if Hoodoo isn't the violent, dangerous, and demonic ritual we're led to believe it is, what is it?

Hoodoo is a folk magic system, meaning that it is a unique practice passed down from generation to generation within a specific culture, in this instance, African American. This practice aims to use charms, spells, and rituals to control the world around the practitioner. Hoodoo has a strong presence in southern black communities, where it is also called "rootwork" and practitioners are called "rootworkers" or "root doctors" rather than the European term "witches." For generations, stretching back to slavery, Hoodoo has existed to provide protection, spiritual and physical healing, and community for African Americans.

Hoodoo is commonly conflated with Voodoo, or the two terms are used interchangeably to refer to any exotic or foreign spirituality. However, the words Hoodoo and

Voodoo evolved separately and are only tenuously related. Voodoo is an organized religion with codified leaders, teachings, and its own pantheon. It's still practiced in many places in the American South and Haiti, and it overlaps with Hoodoo in many ways.

As a folk magic practice, Hoodoo doesn't have much formal organization and isn't strictly tied to a specific religion. Because Christianity has played such an essential role in the lives of enslaved Africans, and thus Hoodoo, many Hoodoo practitioners are Catholic or Protestant. However, it's not necessary. Many practitioners subscribe to West African religious traditions, while others are unaffiliated. Hoodoo is a way for people of any belief system to access the spiritual.

I must note that Hoodoo's history as the spiritual practice of American black folk continues to be important to its practice today. Hoodoo exists because of and for African Americans. It calls upon the power of our enslaved ancestors who suffered at the hand of white oppression. For this reason, Hoodoo is considered a closed practice—meaning it can only be safely and respectfully practiced by descendants of enslaved people.

Respecting closed practices is incredibly important to advancing the lives of oppressed people. African Americans have been stripped of our history and culture. Hoodoo offers us the opportunity to connect to a practice and a way of life that is uniquely and entirely our own, connect with and honor our ancestors, and, most importantly, take control over our lives. That power threatens the forces of white supremacy in America that would seek to destroy our practices and history to assimilate us. This is why Hoodoo is so often demonized, and why it is not respected in the same way as other spiritual and religious practices and ways of life.

However, while a practice can be closed, knowledge is not. Members of any race or ethnicity can and should benefit from educating themselves about Hoodoo. Through studying Hoodoo, you can unlearn the false narratives spread about slavery and the history of black culture. Through this unlearning, you can avoid being complicit in the harmful ideologies that harm not only black people and Hoodoo practitioners but everyone who falls outside of the dominant American culture. An educated ally is a powerful and more empathetic ally.

That is why we are here. Not just to dispel myths but to help guide you through your own spiritual journey. On this journey, you will learn the rich history of Hoodoo in the States, how it came about and took root in America, and what influenced it to become what it is today. You'll learn the core beliefs of Hoodoo and the essential tools a practitioner needs. From there, we'll discuss basic spells and rituals you can use to begin your journey as a Hoodoo practitioner.

All of this new information can be overwhelming, but remember, Hoodoo isn't a strict doctrine nor a science. It is a way of life. I didn't learn about Hoodoo through meticulous study, and neither did any other Hoodoo practitioner. I learned it through watching my grandmother perform rituals on her Altar of the Ancestors, surrounded by fellow family members and the black community of our small southern town. I learned it through the spiritual passion of watching old women shout down the church aisle, overcome by the Holy Spirit. I learned Hoodoo through the people I loved, by using it to forge a path through grief and pain and loss.

Hoodoo has done for me what nothing else could, and it is a tragedy that more people have been dissuaded from embracing this practice to better their own lives because of the lies and sensationalizing of our media. Because of this, I have no choice but to push back against ignorance and misinformation. Do not think of this book as a set of rules or demands. Instead, think of this as an introduction to the next chapter of your own life.

# 1

# A FAR-FROM-BRIEF HISTORY OF HOODOO

There are several reasons why it is challenging to understand the history of Hoodoo. For one, misinformation often outweighs and outnumbers the true history of Hoodoo. The colonialist eye in anthropology and history usually scrubs out the specifics of black culture, either entirely omitting them or boiling them down to something more palatable to white audiences. White supremacy has reasons to want to hide the power and beauty of black spiritual practices, as these inherently push back against our dehumanization.

It's also a struggle because, as a folk magic practice, Hoodoo has not been historically inscribed on paper. This is partly because of enslaved people not being taught to read and write and the ensuing low literacy rates amongst free blacks. However, unlike other oral traditions, Hoodoo was not considered important enough for ruling academics to take the time to record. There is also the desire not to write things down so they cannot be stolen from people outside of the community. This means that many accounts of Hoodoo don't include the voices of actual practitioners and are instead written by outsiders.

Despite the fact that Hoodoo does not conflict with Christianity, Christian culture often demonizes magical practices, meaning Hoodoo often has to be practiced underground in majority Christian black communities. In many Southern towns, sick babies are rushed to rootworkers under the cover of night, their services a poorly kept secret that no one would dare admit in the light of day despite the evidence of their efficacy.

There is also the unfortunate reality that much of our history and connection back to Africa have been lost due to the slave trade. Our storytellers and history keepers died of disease or threw themselves into the ocean, choosing death over enslavement. Our mother tongues were banned and beaten out of us. Our bodies, minds, souls, and spirits were broken, and our culture was permanently damaged.

However, all was not lost. Through perseverance and the power of a tight-knit community, information has survived, and we can still piece together a history of how Hoodoo, as we know it today, came to be.

## THE ORIGINS OF HOODOO

The word "hoodoo" stems from "Hudu," which is the name of a language and tribe that lived in Togo and Ghana and came to America through the transatlantic slave trade first documented in 1875.

The transatlantic slave trade brought an estimated 12 million Africans from their homelands to the Americas between 1514 and 1867. Though it is not often taught in schools, slavery was far more than a mere economic reality or an unfortunate moral blip in America's history. It is among one of the greatest and most vile acts of violence against human beings in recorded history. Slaves were dehumanized in every possible way and forced to survive unimaginable tortures, the first of which was the journey across the middle passage.

The conditions in these slave ships were beyond comprehension. Even if we're taught these realities in school, we often glaze over the human reality. People were packed in like cattle, chained down and forced to lie in their own filth and sick, next to the dead and dying bodies of their fellow man. With each death, another part of African culture was lost, as memories of various cultures, songs, beliefs, practices, and families disappeared. This included the deaths of griots, African storytellers whose very existence centered around keeping the stories, histories, and cultures of tribes alive.

When slaves arrived in the States, they were often forbidden from speaking their native languages. They were given new names, if they were given names at all, and forced into a life of unending labor. Once again, a large amount of information was lost as great minds succumbed to physical and mental torture. Still, somehow bits and pieces of the African religious and spiritual tradition survived, being passed down and morphed through the ever-changing worldview of the American enslaved black folk.

In the midst of great suffering, it is human nature to seek higher meaning and control. For people who are entirely disempowered in the physical world, their only escape is the spiritual. Enslaved black people went to great lengths to hold onto their spiritual practices even as white slave owners tried to crack down on them. To combat this, slaves took their spiritual practices to isolated areas, praying into pots to muffle the sounds of their worship.

The Bible was just as important as the whip to the slave owner. By twisting scripture and selectively preaching to slaves, they could attack the spirit of these people and convince them that they deserved their place as cattle. In Louisiana, laws known as Code Noir were put in place to forbid slaves from practicing anything other than Catholicism. On some plantations, churches were run by slave preachers who white overseers heavily monitored. Still, these black congregations managed to hide messages of freedom and dignity in plain sight.

They also absorbed Christianity into their spiritual practices, effectively cloaking their religion under the guise of assimilation. While slave masters preached verses that venerated submission and the ideals of slavery, black folk latched onto the story of Moses freeing his people from the promised land. Outside of Hoodoo, the story of Moses is still significant to black people, but it holds a special place in the Hoodoo worldview.

Hoodoo is a syncretic belief, meaning it finds unity amongst different beliefs and practices. This is what makes it uniquely accessible to people of various belief systems. These cultural influences relate to the black population moving from Africa to American plantations, and then across the United States after emancipation.

### African

The vast majority of these enslaved people were kidnapped from West Africa and were members of a few specific ethnic groups, including the Kongo, Yoruba, Ewe, and Igbo people. Plants and herbs play an essential part in Hoodoo, and many plants were brought over from Africa during the slave trade. Some even wore amulets with licorice seed on the slave ships for protection. The spiritual practices and beliefs that later defined the African American experience are uniquely Central and West African.

### West Africa

One of the major religions in West Africa was Islam, and many people had belief systems that combined Islam and African spiritualism. West African conjurers often dressed in more Islamic clothing, which identified them to other enslaved people as being able to provide protection through conjuring or witchcraft.

The Mandingo or Mandinka people were among one of the first primarily Muslim groups brought to America with their gris-gris bags, now known as mojo bags, which were used for protection. Many carried their gris-gris bags with them aboard slave ships.

The Yoruba people brought with them the importance of crossroads, often performing rituals at crossroads, as they believed the trickster deity Eshu-Elegba resided there. This continued to be important in Hoodoo, as they symbolize a point of transition and can be used in spells. There are places in Louisiana and Africa where you can find offerings placed at intersections for this reason.

The Igbo people brought with them the practice of having two burial ceremonies, one for the physical body and the second for mourning and celebrating that person's life, a practice which persists today in African American culture through homegoing ceremonies. It is even suspected that President James Madison was poisoned by his Igbo slaves using herbal magic.

### ▸ Central Africa

Artifacts of Central African spiritual beliefs have been found all over the slave-owning South. Charms like beads, seashells, polished stones, and bones were used by slaves descending from Central Africa for protection.

The Bantu-Kongo people brought with them the Kongo Cosmogram. This symbol depicts the sun's rising and setting, the boundaries between the physical and spiritual world, and the power of God flowing into the realm of the ancestors. The cosmogram is important to the Bantu-Kongo practices surrounding communication with ancestors.

The First African Baptist Church, a historic landmark that was a stop on the Underground Railroad, has a cosmogram punctured in the basement. Images of the cosmogram can be found in several historically black churches across the South. The Bantu-Kongo people also had Minkisis, singular Nkisis, which are hand-made objects possessed by a spirit or multiple spirits, often in the form of mojo or conjure bags. They also used conjure canes, staffs used in healing or conjuring rituals.

One of the most noticeable Hoodoo practices, specifically in the rural South, hails from the Bantu-Kongo people. This is the use of bottle trees. Originally, the Bantu-Kongo people would decorate yards and entryways with shiny, broken items to ward off evil spirits. This evolved in the Americas as hanging glass bottles outside one's house as a form of protection.

### Native American

By the 1700s, the population of black folks and Native Americans combined outnumbered whites in the South. For this reason, the colonizers had good reason to fear the two groups revolting against the oppressive powers and sought to prevent contact between the two groups as much as they could. However, black and Native populations continued to intermingle and share many of their cultural and spiritual practices. This took the form of intermarriage and Native Americans holding African slaves. However, the native people had a differing view of slavery when compared to their white counterparts, and these enslaved people were often later adopted into the tribe.

Enslaved Africans were influenced by the herbal practices of Native Americans for both medicinal and spiritual purposes. Those who used healing practices that stemmed from the Native Americans were among some of the most sought-after healers in times of crisis. For example, both the Native Americans and black folks believed puccoon root could bring good luck if rubbed, red pepper could provide protection, and the Adam and Eve root could bring love.

One example of the relationship between Hoodoo, enslaved Africans, and Native Seminoles is the Seminole nation, located in Florida. During the early 1800s, the Seminoles warred against the United States, as they housed many escaped slaves. It's said they were aided by an escaped Hoodoo conjurer named Uncle Monday, who refused to relocate to Native American Territory along with the Seminoles and other escaped slaves, instead fleeing in the form of an alligator.

### *European*

There are many similarities between European witchcraft and African conjure, such as divination, fortune-telling, and the use of charms. Both rely on the belief that humans have the ability to manipulate the spiritual world to influence the physical. Just like Celtic pagans, African Vodou practitioners had to accommodate the force of Christianity. Some Hoodoo practitioners work with European deities, such as the Greek or Celtic pantheon.

The use of candles in spiritual altars is borrowed from European practices. Many Hoodoo conjurers get their ritual candles from Jewish shops. Some Hoodoo practitioners adopted the practice of covering or turning mirrors following a death, believing that a mirror could be tainted by reflecting the image of a corpse. The influence of European practices was a mix of both purposeful exchange as well as forced assimilation.

## FROM VOODOO TO HOODOO

The modern word "Voodoo" stems from the West African religion "Vodou." Modern Voodoo is primarily practiced in Haiti and Louisiana. While many people incorrectly call Voodoo a polytheistic religion, it is more accurate to say that it is a diffused monotheistic religion, meaning they believe in a singular supreme God as well as several lesser Gods. One thing Hoodoo shares with Voodoo is the focus on doing rather than scripture or doctrine.

### Yoruba

Vodou can be traced back to the Yoruba people, specifically as they were the majority of the slaves shipped to Haiti. These West African religious beliefs evolved into their own unique religion. There are several reasons for this, one of which was the fact that while the Americas were primarily protestant, Catholicism was the ruling doctrine in Haiti. Slaves were forbidden from practicing their native religions. However, the presence of the Saints in Catholicism allowed enslaved Africans a way to hide their worship of spirits, known as the Lwa or Loa. They assigned specific Loa to the Saints to both assimilate and maintain their beliefs. However, protestant Christianity warns heavily against idol worship, making this sort of assimilation difficult in the States.

Another reason for the differences between Hoodoo and Voodoo is that the slave population of the Caribbean was also far denser than in the Americas. Smaller populations of slaves were easier for white overseers to control, and thus it was easier to squash their native practices. Caribbean slaves were also generally in poorer health and reproduced less often. Meanwhile, in the Americas, there were far more blacks born into slavery with no connection to their African roots.

## THE COLORS OF HOODOO

Hoodoo is the result of the survival instinct of enslaved black folks surviving even as its original religious roots were destroyed. Engrained in Hoodoo is the need of our enslaved ancestors to protect themselves, physically and spiritually, while enduring the unimaginable horror of slavery. It could be said that African Americans would not have been able to survive and thrive in the way we have, to create our beautiful, rich, and powerful modern history without the influence of Hoodoo. Hoodoo resonated with slaves as it allowed them to take control over their lives and environments when the entire structure of the country they resided in was designed to strip them of all power.

Hoodoo is open to only the descendants of slaves. For someone who does not descend from slaves, who has not been affected by this specific oppression, to practice Hoodoo would be not only disrespectful but dangerous, as they lack the support and presence of the ancestors Hoodoo draws from.

Hoodoo being a closed practice does not mean that non-black people have no access to the spiritual realm. People of European ancestry have many different religious, spiritual, and folk magic practices available to them. If a white person does not have enough knowledge of their ethnic history to research the folk magic of their ancestors, it is because white supremacy harms everyone. White immigrants, such as the Irish, were forced to abandon their native practices in order to be brought into white culture. I would encourage any white person who is inspired by Hoodoo to seek the magic of their own culture.

## THE RECLAIMING OF HOODOO CULTURE

Hoodoo has never gone away, but while it has been forced to exist in the shadows to avoid persecution, in recent years there has been a significant resurgence in loud and proud practitioners. This shift has somewhat coincided with a general cultural interest in witchcraft. Because most of the modern representation of witchcraft has been dominated by white witches, Hoodoo practitioners have stepped up to spread knowledge about this unique practice. This push for awareness and acceptance has also gone hand-in-hand with black feminism, as many Hoodoo practitioners, especially young ones, are women.

Black practitioners have been working diligently to educate people about the truth of Hoodoo and bring attention to its rich and long history to make it known that Hoodoo isn't just a trend. It's something that runs in the veins of all black folks. For many people, it isn't something new. Instead, they are loudly and publicly embracing for the first time the practices they saw their parents, grandparents, and great-grandparents do in secret.

This reclamation has taken many forms. With the help of artist and illustrator Stephanie Singleton, Actress Rachel True has created a set of Tarot cards that depict black women. In contrast, most other cards have a decidedly European lean. Others have organized meetups, festivals, and groups specifically for African American magic practitioners. All of this vital work serves to destigmatize the world of Hoodoo and send a clear message to black folks who are looking to take the first step into folk magic: there is a place for you here, and there always has been.

## CONCLUSION

African American history cannot be separated from Hoodoo and vice versa. In order to understand one, you must understand the other. From the beginning of the slave trade to the modern-day, Hoodoo has persisted as a way for marginalized people to access their higher selves and serve their communities when no one else would. The very fact that Hoodoo has survived this long, just like African Americans, seems like a testament to the supernatural in and of itself.

2

# HOODOO BELIEFS

As Hoodoo is an old and complicated practice, the specific beliefs of Hoodoo are rich and complex. Each practitioner will have a unique relationship to the spiritual world filtered through their own beliefs. However, Hoodoo is guided by a few immutable principles that inform the worldview and morality of its practitioners. Without these beliefs, whatever witchcraft you perform isn't Hoodoo.

## HOODOO AND CHRISTIANITY

One of the biggest hurdles to coming to understand Hoodoo is cultural Christianity. Even for those who are no longer believers or even those who were never raised Christian, Christian beliefs, ways of thinking, and attitudes permeate our culture and affect everyone. Despite the aversion to witchcraft in Christian spaces, the Bible itself actually has many instances of practices that we would call witchcraft today that are ordained by God. Using holy oils, divination through dreams, incense burning, and herbal potions frequently appear throughout.

Many Hoodoo practitioners are Christian, and Christianity profoundly influenced the development of Hoodoo. Many spells and rituals listed in the literature about Hoodoo call for the use of the Bible, Catholic and protestant prayers and practices, and Christian imagery like crosses.

However, the way that modern Christianity is practiced in the West is often very different from older religious practices. Much of how we practice Christianity in the States is more cultural than it is biblical. Deconstructing these beliefs and identifying the similarities and differences between Hoodoo and Christianity is an essential step in the journey of becoming a practitioner.

### *God*

God, as commonly understood in mainstream Christianity, is omnipotent and omniscient. He controls everything. Everything is laid out in his plans. This means that humans have little to no autonomy and thus cannot exercise their own will over the spiritual. Mainstream Christians often see prayer as a request, not as a force in and of itself. They wait for God to act on their behalf.

In Hoodoo, however, humans can act on behalf of the supreme deity and control the spiritual world of their own accord. And acts achieved through conjuring are still seen as God's will, as God is still in everything. Many Hoodoo practitioners believe in the God represented in African traditions; a genderless, morally neutral, and uninvolved God. Because God does not concern himself with the goings-on of humans, we access lesser spirits.

## Spirits

Christianity and Hoodoo also share similar beliefs about spirits, that they can possess a persona and affect them physically. We see this often in black churches. This can take the form of catching the Holy Spirit or demonic possession. American Christian spirit possession bears a striking resemblance to the spirit possession seen in Voodoo ceremonies, including eyes rolling back, jerking, ecstatic movement, and babbling.

However, these beliefs diverge when it comes to the specifics of these spirits. Hoodoo and Vodou recognize the Lwa or Loa. Christian Hoodoo practitioners often associate the Lwa with angels or Saints. There are not separate gods but manifestations of the one God. These spirits are connected to different things, places, acts, and people and move throughout the world similarly to humans, pursuing their own goals based on their emotions. They allow the divine creator to be closer to us. They allow us to comprehend the spiritual.

While it is said that there are thousands of Lwa, at least 232 of them have been named. Each Lwa has its own personality and is associated with different colors and objects. Hoodoo practitioners can communicate with and interact with these spirits through their practice. You can call spirits into a place or create a barrier that they cannot pass. If you use them to complete a spell, they will expect to be paid through offerings. Pleasing the Lwa through ritual, divination, and offering can provide a practitioner with protection, assistance, and wisdom. Likewise, offending a Lwa can result in serious affliction. The spirits of Hoodoo can also be understood as belonging to three main groups.

### ▸ Spirits of Roots

Hoodoo practices utilize naturally occurring elements like roots and herbs to allow someone to influence both the physical and the spiritual. It can be difficult in our modern age to reconnect with nature. Still, when you do, and you experience the inherent connection that we as human beings have to the Earth, you can recognize just how much power we have growing all around us.

Each plant has its own unique spirit and its own abilities. Some can bring luck, love, friendship, and happiness into our lives. Others can give us a gateway into the spiritual world. There can be overlap between the spirits of different plants, but there is also great nuance that can only be learned through careful practice and attention.

### ▸ Spirits of Earth

Spirits of Earth refer to the properties of the ground given to it by its proximity to something else. The environment is absorbent, and we can utilize the spirits that it absorbs—using Earth that has absorbed the properties associated with what we want out of a ritual grounds us and helps us avoid getting unexpected results. Whether the Earth you use is from a church or a prison, barren or fertile, from a garden or a grave, will affect the results of your divination. Using soil in rituals also grounds us and keeps our rituals controlled and stable.

### ▸ Ancestral Spirits

In the Bible, we see many instances of the importance of ancestry and bloodlines. Referring to the Christian God as "The God of Abraham, Isaac, and Jacob," Moses returning to protect his blood-related people, and, most importantly, the curse of man brought on us by the sins of Adam and Eve all exalt the importance of one's family line. However, there is often little talk of one's lineage in modern Christianity, discarded in favor of individualism.

Christianity regards death as a permanent disconnection from the physical world. When a person dies, their entire spiritual being is taken to Heaven, and we can't interact with them until we die ourselves. However, in Hoodoo, we believe that while the soul of the person goes to be with God, the spirit remains where we can interact and communicate with them.

In Hoodoo, one's ancestors are essential. For many African Americans, we are the descendants of slaves whose family line was never recorded. For many of us, the only way we can connect to our ancestors is through the spiritual realm. Our DNA carries with it the stories, suffering, triumphs, and spirits of the people who created us. Our ancestry is how we come to know ourselves, and only by understanding ourselves can we hope to utilize our full spiritual abilities. A person's ancestry can manifest in many ways, from bad luck to compulsive behaviors and emotions.

Communicating with our ancestors can provide us with wisdom we would otherwise go without. They know things that we don't. They've experienced things we could never imagine. They can explain to us the curses or rewards placed on our family lines by their actions and explain our circumstances. Our ancestors are far more willing to help and guide us than other spirits, though we must first acknowledge and respect them.

### *Moses*

The story of Moses freeing the slaves from Egypt continues to be important in black spiritual culture. In Hoodoo, Moses is considered to be the best Hoodoo conjurer in history. His performance of miracles is in line with Hoodoo conjuring, as he accessed the spiritual and the supernatural to enact the will of God and enact his own will on the world around him.

Just as Moses was an instrument of God, so are other Hoodoo conjures. However, magic is forbidden by the Mosaic law. This is because Moses sought to restrict magical practices to priests. There are many instances in the Bible of what we might now call Hoodoo or rootwork that were not considered blasphemous, as it was authorized by the church. King David is given a message from God through the stones on a priest's breastplate. In Numbers, it is outlined how a priest may cause a pregnant woman to have an abortion using bitter water.

### The Bible

The Psalms are often used as spells or ritual words which were spoken during spellcasting, as they reflect both the intent of the conjurer and call upon God. The Bible also holds magical power in and of itself. It can be used as a talisman of protection and is often placed on ancestral altars.

## GRAVEYARDS

One of the most controversial, poorly understood, and unique elements of Hoodoo is the relationship with graves and graveyards. Western media often depicts graveyards as a fearful and evil place, making those who willingly enter them for spiritual purposes evil or demonic. Graveyards often go hand-in-hand with imagery of devil worship, human sacrifice, and all of the awful stereotypes about Hoodoo and Voodoo you can think of. Part of this is because of how taboo the subject of death often is in the West. We do our best to avoid talking about or even thinking about death. Hoodoo, however, regards death as a natural and beautiful part of the order of things; it is not an end, but a transformation.

Graves are monuments to our love of the people who have passed. They are sites at which the spiritual power of our ancestors combines with the power of the Earth. They are places of transition from one state to another. They are incredibly powerful places. Hoodoo practitioners might perform rituals in a graveyard or use soil from a grave in their divination. However, while you can do amazing things through graveyard magic, there are also dangers you need to be aware of, which is why many experienced Hoodoo practitioners would advise against beginners jumping headlong into graveyard magic.

There are several things you must keep in mind. Firstly, the Earth is absorbent, and if you're collecting soil from a grave, you have to be aware of who that person was. Your results will vary depending on whether you're using the grave of a serial killer or a nurse, or an oil baron. You must have the intuition and spiritual sensitivity to communicate with the spirits around you well enough that you know who you're working with. It's also important to be respectful, both to the people around you and to the spirit. It's essential to communicate to the spirit of the deceased. You should also not take soil from a grave without a trade or payment, such as libations or food.

## SIX PRINCIPLES OF HOODOO

There are six guiding ideologies that are important in any and every act of Hoodoo magic.

### Intention

Your personal desires for the outcome of a ritual as well as God's desire is of supreme importance. A curse laid down for one person will only affect that one person. God will also not allow curses to work on an undeserving or incorrect target. When practicing Hoodoo, it is essential to focus on your intentions and have a clear idea of what your desires are. Without a clear head, your results could be chaotic.

### Divination

Hoodoo practitioners can access and communicate with spirits and glean their knowledge. This grants us clairvoyance and the ability to see realities of both the present and past. We can reveal information about the true nature of things and happenings outside of our earthly eye.

### The Divine Providence

There is a Higher Power, a spiritual being that many of us refer to as God, that is directly involved and invested in the goings-on of the physical world. Hoodoo practitioners can abide by any religion, and thus, worship and address any number of deities.

### *Principles of Signatures*

The Higher Power designed everything with a purpose. Every element and every person has a mark that assigns it its place in the universe. We can see this mark through careful observation.

### *Vengeful Justice*

Unlike other religions, spiritual beliefs, or magic systems that cling to the importance of doing no harm, Hoodoo accepts harm in the form of fair retribution. This doesn't include doing unearned harm to a person, but if someone slights you, you can use Hoodoo to get revenge or offensively protect yourself. The harm done through Hoodoo must be proportionate to the harm incurred.

### *After Life*

Death is not the end but a transition into a new state of being. Our soul continues on after our bodily death. Through this continued life, we can communicate with our blood ancestors. They can look after us, inform us, and intercede in our lives.

## CONCLUSION

While the spirituality of Hoodoo might seem vague from the outside, it is only because it is incredibly complex and challenging to explain with mere words. Much of Hoodoo spirituality is meant to be experienced and explored rather than objectively discussed by scholars. At its core, Hoodoo believes that God is in everything, and we can access God through anything. When we do, we open ourselves up to our true power.

3

# THE ESSENTIAL TOOLS OF HOODOO PRACTITIONERS

You don't need a big budget to practice Hoodoo. Hoodoo was meant to be practiced by people who had very little, who were isolated, and who had no core church or coven to run to. The tools of Hoodoo do not have magical power by themselves. They are instead the means through which you access the spiritual. By properly using these tools, you'll be able to start utilizing the spiritual in your everyday life.

## ALTAR

There are two types of altars. The first is a ritual altar, which we will discuss later. These are used to perform specific spells and are broken down afterward. Often overlooked, however, is the ancestral altar, and this is arguably the most crucial element of being a practitioner. The ancestral altar also overlaps with the spiritual altar, meant to contact deities rather than dead relatives, and they are constructed in much the same way.

Our ancestors are our most powerful resource in Hoodoo, and you must maintain a direct and intimate relationship with them. You need your ancestors not only to provide you with power in your rituals but to guide you, to help you avoid pitfalls and negative situations, to provide you with strength and wisdom, and to connect you to who you are.

Ancestral veneration is such a foreign concept in many Western spaces, and there is also a lot of misinformation and contradictory advice regarding how one should interact with their ancestors. Many novice practitioners skip connecting with their ancestors altogether so they can "get to the good stuff." However, any magic you do without the help of your ancestors is a shot in the dark and can put you in grave danger. Your blood is who you are, and there is no way to tap into your true power without first knowing who you are. If you really want to maximize your abilities as a Hoodoo practitioner, you have to start with connecting to your ancestors, and you do this through your altar.

**How to Build Your Ancestral Altar**

Your altar is the point at which you access your ancestors, so you'll want to place it in a part of your home that has little traffic. Think of it as setting up a sort of guest suite for your relatives. It should be in a private place where few people will be passing through, such as a separate room or a closet if necessary. It's essential your altar isn't in the space where you sleep, as the spiritual traffic can affect your sleep patterns and dreams.

- **Basic Altar**

Your altar can be any size and can be a table or on the floor of a shelf. What's important is that the base of your altar is made of something natural—wood being the most accessible. You can try setting up your altar low to the ground so that you can kneel before it, as kneeling is a great way to show respect for your ancestors and deities.

Once you've set up the base for your altar, you'll need to clean it with a spiritual liquid. Some may use holy water. Others may use Florida Water, a Hoodoo staple. Originally, Florida Water was a cologne named after the supposed fountain of youth located in Florida that was used by house slaves. Kolonia 1800 also has a similar history and a similar use as a spiritual cleanser. When you clean your altar space, use circular, clockwise motions. You can then anoint your altar with oil, which we will discuss in further detail later on.

Now that your altar space is cleaned, say a prayer over the area. Express your desires for the space, how you want it to be a holy and spiritual area. Remember, intention is critical.

You can also take this time to bless your altar space with oils, which we will discuss.

Cover your altar with a cloth. While altars made for specific spells might call for cloths of a particular color, such as green for money spells or red for love spells, you can be creative with your cloth on your ancestral altar. You'll want something natural, like cotton or wool.

Place a Bible front and center on your altar. Not only will your Bible provide you with powerful spells, but your Christian ancestors will respond to familiar verses. You're going to be adding more objects, so make sure your Bible doesn't take up the entire altar.

To illuminate the space for your ancestors and guide them to you, you'll add a white seven-day candle. You'll be using different colored candles for various purposes throughout your Hoodoo journey, but because white is the most basic color and it provides clarity, purity, protection, and peace, you'll want it to be the staple of your ancestral altar. You'll light this once your entire altar is set up, and it will stay lit at all times, so get several of them.

Fill a glass with water and place it next to a candle. This refers to the transition between life and death as we enter the world of the living through the water of the womb, and bodies of water, in general, are seen as representing these transitions.

Lastly, place pictures of your ancestors on both sides of your Bible. This is the most basic altar setup, and if this is all you can do, your ancestors will understand, and you will still be able to facilitate a relationship with them. However, there are other steps and other objects that you can add to your altar to intensify this connection.

- **Enhancing Your Altar**

Any objects that belonged to your ancestors will improve its efficacy. These should be placed in front of their pictures. The most important thing to include is offerings. This is to both show respect for your ancestors and draw them to you. Coffee, alcohol, and food are very common.

You can also add any items that are important in your spiritual journey. Divination tools like oils, crystals, bones, or tarot cards can all have a place on your altar if they are important to you as a Hoodoo practitioner. You'll be able to use these to specify and clarify any messages you receive from your ancestors through your altar.

Another essential addition to an altar is an image of a spirit of protection. More experienced Hoodoo practitioners will choose a spirit they have worked within the past, but if you're a beginner, you can select a spirit you feel drawn to. For example, if you're working with the Catholic Saints, you might choose Archangel Michael or The Virgin Mary. However, if you're working with the Loa, you might be drawn to Erzulie Dantor. The reason you want to include this spirit of protection is to filter out and protect you from any harmful spiritual energy that might enter into your life through your altar. Give your spirit of protection its own candle and glass of water.

Some other items you might want to include are the soil from the grave of an ancestor, flowers, incense or oil burners, a bell, or some spiritual cleansing liquid. Your ancestral altar is incredibly personal and should reflect your unique relationship and respect for your ancestors.

- **Caring for Your Altar**

Your altar is how you show respect for your ancestors, and the state you keep it in reflects that respect. Replace your offerings once a week, make sure it is cleaned as described above, and keep your candle lit at all times. You also need to take great care that the area of your altar is spiritually and energetically cleansed and pure. While using purifying and cleansing oils and incense will deal with the area and the physical items on your altar, you yourself might still carry negative energy that needs to be dealt with through spiritually cleansing yourself, as we will later discuss.

- **Working at Your Altar**

Your altar isn't a passive thing but a space for you to connect and communicate with your ancestors, so you'll need to use it regularly. At the beginning of your journey, this may take time and effort, but eventually, communicating with your ancestors will become a natural and intuitive part of your life.

One common practice in both Hoodoo and many other magical and religious belief systems is the covering or veiling of hair. For some, this relates to modesty. Others believe that their hair carries magical significance. Either way, if it is comfortable for you, veiling might be an excellent way to show respect and veneration for your ancestors when you come before your altar.

When you first set up your altar, you'll want to invite your ancestors to it using a three-day ritual.

**Day One:** Set aside a period of time when you can focus solely on this. Go to your altar and think of your ancestors, the memories you have of them, their faces, the joy and love you shared with them, and the respect you have for them. Say a prayer to them. Speak their names. It might take time for you to establish this connection with them, but you need to make it known that you are there, ready, and able to connect with them. You can also do things like visiting their graves or meditating on things that were beloved by them.

**Day Two:** Share a meal with them that they would like. Cook for two and make a plate for them. Set one plate on the altar and, as you eat, think of your ancestors, pray, and meditate as you did before. Leave the food on your altar until it is stale.

**Day Three:** Bring a gift for your ancestors. This can be anything like food, cigars, alcohol, or perfume. Try to make these gifts personal. Now is the time to light your altar candle and meditate once more. Remember, your ancestors fought through unimaginable hardship so that you could live. You are the culmination of all of their hard work, suffering, joys, and heartbreak. Show them you are grateful for the life you have due to their sacrifices. Talk to your ancestors out loud and offer them worship. You can sing, dance, paint, wave flags, anything to express your gratitude for them and their attention.

Now that your ancestors have been invited, you have to honor that invitation by spending time with them each day. Make this a part of your daily routine and build prayers and worship into your schedule. After some time of dutiful attention, your ancestors will start to communicate with you and answer your prayers. Be loyal and patient.

## INCENSE

Incense has many uses. No matter what you're doing, be it a particular ritual or just spending time with your ancestors, your practice can benefit from the use of incense. Any incense will have a unique blend of herbs and oils, and these oils have unique purposes and connections. Make sure to do some research about the particular incense you're using so you can utilize it to the best of your abilities.

Firstly, incense is calming and can create the specific atmosphere you're looking for during your practice. Something like lavender can be used if you're struggling to relax and it's affecting your focus. You can also burn incense that reminds you of certain people, places, or things related to the ritual you're doing.

You can use incense to purify people, places, and things of negative energies and evil. Simply spread the smoke out over the item you want to purify. Sandalwood, Frankincense, and White Copal are popular purifiers.

When praying, incense can be used to enhance and intensify your prayers, as it is believed the smoke carries your prayers up to the heavens. Incense can also be used as an offering or sacrifice to your ancestors or the deities you're working with.

## HOODOO DOLLS

Whatever you've seen about Voodoo dolls in the media, throw it out. Hoodoo dolls are another element of Hoodoo that have been appropriated and misrepresented so much that the false narrative has come to dominate cultural consciousness. In reality, Hoodoo dolls are a means of using the spiritual realm to manipulate the physical. There are three main guiding principles that dictate this.

The first is sympathetic magic. Sympathetic magic is based on the principle that all things are connected through invisible bonds and that by tapping into these connections, we can manipulate our physical reality.

The second is homeopathic energy which says that like things attract one another. For example, if you make a wax likeness of a person, you can cause that person harm or death by melting the wax image and utilizing their attracted fates.

The third is contagious magic. Things that come into contact with one another will forever be connected to each other. You can affect one thing by manipulating something it once came into contact with. You might be able to gain control or influence over someone by getting your hands on their hair, teeth, or waste. You could heal a wound by manipulating the thing that caused that wound.

Hoodoo dolls work based on these principles. They give the practitioner a physical item that allows them to manipulate something else through spiritual bonds.

**Types of Hoodoo Dolls**

Depending on the goals of the practitioner, there are four different types of Hoodoo dolls that can be used for various purposes and require their own unique care, construction, and intent.

- **Spirit Dolls**

Spirit dolls are vessels for a spirit. This can be any spirit, be it a Lwa, an ancestor, or a deity. Spirit dolls are often used on altars and receive sacrifices, offerings, worship, and devotion so that the practitioner might utilize their power and influence.

- **Helper Dolls**

These dolls represent a specific thing the practitioner wants to attract. A helper doll could represent wealth, love, power, happiness, or whatever it is the practitioner is currently working toward. Their construction will represent this concept. They're usually the color associated with the thing the practitioner wants to attract and can be stuffed with specific roots or herbs that are correctly associated. For example, a helper doll for attracting love might be made of red or pink cloth.

- **Doll Babies**

Doll Babies bear the most resemblance to the media's representation of a "voodoo doll" as they are created to represent an individual rather than a spirit or a concept. Like helper dolls, their construction reflects their specific purpose. At the very least, they'll include a piece of paper with the person's name on it, but they can also be made out of the possessions of that individual. They can also be a particular color that reflects the practitioner's intent and might be made to look like the individual or have a picture of that person's face taped to their head.

- **Effigies**

Effigies are similar to doll babies, but instead of being made to represent any person, effigies represent you, the practitioner. You can use these to care for yourself and use the spiritual to affect your physical self. An effigy should be treated with the utmost love, care, and attention, never left unattended for too long, and stored in a safe place, wrapped in a white cloth.

**How to Make a Hoodoo Doll**

There are several options for making a Hoodoo doll. What you choose to do should depend on your goals, your access to materials, and, of course, your intuition. While making your Hoodoo doll, make sure to keep your mind focused on your intent, your desires, and the person or spirit your doll is supposed to be connected to.

- **Store-bought**

You can use a store-bought doll as the base of your Hoodoo doll. This might be especially helpful if you're trying to make a doll baby or effigy, and you find a store-bought doll that looks exactly like you or another person. You can also find custom Hoodoo doll makers on many craft sites such as Etsy. After purchasing your doll, you'll want to first make sure it is cleansed. Then, incorporate items that relate to the particular person, spirit, or concept you're trying to work with.

- **Wax Images**

For wax images, you can use regular candles or male and female candles for added specificity. Be conscious of the color of the candle you choose. Start by scratching the name you want to be associated with your doll into the candle. Then, create a hole in the bottom and fill it with related items and reseal the hole with wax.

- **Poppets**

Poppets are hand-made dolls created by two pieces of fabric into the shape of a human body. The material your poppet is made of is important and can reflect not only the person the poppet is meant to represent but your goals for them. You can use items that belong to a specific person, such as a piece of clothing. You can also use things that relate to your desires for that person. If you're making an effigy for your own sexual health, you might use a piece of lingerie. We'll dive more in-depth into color theory later on, but I'll mention that it can be very powerful in your poppet construction. Using green fabric for wealth or red fabric for protection will help enhance your intentions.

Once you've sewn the basic shape, customize it as much as possible. Hair color, eye color, body type, and unique markings can all be taken into account when customizing your doll. You can also include physical items that bind the doll to the individual, such as a taglock. Taglock refers to a physical piece of a person, such as a matted clump of hair, fingernails, or even bodily fluids. Including these will only strengthen the connection. Once done, wrap your doll in a clean cloth while you aren't using it in your rituals.

**Baptizing Your Doll**

Once your doll has been constructed, you have one last step before it's ready to be used in your rituals, and that is baptism. This process is also sometimes called ritual naming. This is where the deity of your doll is sealed, and the connection is established. Sprinkle or bathe it with holy water or a spiritual liquid while repeating the name of the spirit, person, or concept that you want to be imbued into it. You'll also want to say a prayer over the doll, talking about your intentions and its name. You can also leave your doll resting on an appropriate picture overnight.

**Disposing of Your Doll**

Once your Hoodoo doll has served its purpose, you must release its spirit and connection to its person and lay it to rest respectfully. To do this, make the symbol of the cross over your chest and say a prayer releasing the spirit, such as: "Allow my words that connect you to set you free so that you may return to where you came from. In the name of the Father, the Son, and of the Holy Spirit. Amen."

Once the spirit has been released, you can choose to burn it, give it a burial, throw it in running water, or leave it at a crossroads. Seek out the guidance of your ancestors and deities if you aren't sure what exactly to do with it.

**Basic Hoodoo Doll Ingredients**

If you're going the route of entirely constructing your own poppet, here are a few examples of what might go into poppets with different uses. Feel free to change or add to these ritual items as long as your choices are purposeful, and you're communicating with your deities and ancestors about it.

- **Love Poppet**

A love poppet can be for yourself or for your beloved. Include a picture of the targeted person, a taglock, as well as ginger, rose petals, orris root, vanilla beans, peppermint, and carnelian stones. Make the body of your poppet out of red or pink fabric. You can also make two poppets, one for you and one for your beloved, then tie them together using red or pink string.

- **Employment Poppet**

If you're seeking employment or a better job, use green or gold fabric to make the body of your doll. Stuff it with tonka beans, cloves, ginger, nutmeg, and cinnamon as well as tourmaline or citrine. Include any items related to why you would be a great candidate along with your picture and/or taglock.

- **Protection Poppet**

Use white fabric for a protection poppet. Include herbs like basil, juniper, mandrake, cope, and frankincense as well as onyx or quartz stones. While creating this, visualize a bubble of brilliant light surrounding you or the target and acting as a shield.

- **Family Protection Poppets**

Use modeling clay to make poppets of each of your family members. Press stones such as hematite, black onyx, and amethyst as well as herbs like basil, coffee beans, and patchouli into the wet clay. Store these in a safe place in your home and surround them with a circle of protection.

- **Stop the Gossip Poppet**

Mold the body of your poppet out of soft meat, like ground beef or pork. Include horseradish, pepper, rue yarrow, and valerian root. As you do, state your intentions. Tell the poppet it is time to stop talking and spreading stories. Once you're done, you can dispose of it by burning it or leaving it out to rot.

- **Healing Poppet**

Make the body of your healing poppet with blue or white fabric. Include a bloodstone as well as wintergreen, rose, carnation, ivy, pine, or lemon balms. It's essential to be specific about the ailment you wish to heal, so focus your mind and intentions on that issue.

- **Poppet in a Pinch**

If you find yourself in immediate need of a poppet, use aluminum foil to form into the shape of the targeted person. Fill it with any magical items you can find nearby like kitchen herbs, wood, petition papers, or soil.

CONCLUSION

These tools are precious to a Hoodoo practitioner and should be treated with the utmost respect. Make sure you keep your tools clean and spiritually cleansed. You should also be paying consistent attention to your tools. With Hoodoo dolls specifically, make sure the way you treat them reflects your goals and intent. Simply following the recipes by the letter and then abandoning them will not grant you any spiritual power.

# 4

# ROOTWORK

For enslaved Africans and black folks who lived in the rural South, the only access to medical attention they could get was through the Earth in the form of rootwork. Rootwork taps into the natural power that exists in all the gifts of Mother Nature. Hoodoo became known as Rootwork precisely because of its uses of roots and herbs, though some use the term to refer specifically to rituals that include plants.

Much of this knowledge was brought over from Africa to the States, where most healing was done chemically rather than herbally. White slaveholders often feared being poisoned by their slaves because of this rich herbal knowledge. Laws were passed to prevent enslaved black folks from practicing or administering medicine for this very reason. Enslaved women used herbs to control their fertility and cause miscarriages to prevent children from suffering slavery. This developed into an intrinsic connection between black midwives and Hoodoo. To this day, African American women struggle to find suitable natal care in the mainstream medical field. Black midwives and Hoodoo practitioners offered not only powerful herbal medicine but compassion and care that could not be found anywhere else.

Hoodoo healers are often called root doctors. This term is incredibly important but also informal. As this knowledge was passed down from generation to generation rather than formalized, there is no school or body of singular knowledge that can make someone a root doctor. To be called a root doctor, a person would need to be accepted by the community as such and recognized by other root doctors as capable of giving people the help they need.

Hoodoo overlaps with homeopathy but takes it a step further. Hoodoo isn't just concerned with the physical healing properties of plants but the spiritual properties as well. Part of becoming a Hoodoo practitioner is being comfortable and knowledgeable about these unique properties.

## GETTING YOUR HERBS

Like many things in life, what's convenient isn't always best, and what's best isn't always convenient. For simple spells, you can take the route of buying herbs from the store that have been commercially grown and processed, and you can even get decent results. Keep in mind where and how these herbs were grown, picked, and processed, as unethical practices might come with negative energy.

However, if your goal is to make Hoodoo a long-term part of your life, and if you want to fully invest in this spiritual journey, you'll want to put more thought and effort into cultivating the herbs you use.

### *Foraging/Wildcrafting*

Foraging offers you the most powerful yield, as it is absolutely and completely connected to nature. Foraging, also known as wildcrafting, is not only a great way to get powerful herbs but can also be a tremendous and meditative practice that can help you connect to your deeper self away from the bustle and distraction of modern life.

However, foraging can be dangerous for beginners if you don't do prior research. You don't want to end up picking, ingesting, or burning poisonous herbs. If you do go the route of foraging, go with a more experienced forager, or seek out a guide that instructs you on how to know similar plants apart from each other. It would be best if you also kept in mind the laws in your area, so you don't end up foraging on private land, and be familiar with the unique flora of your region. It's also good form to only pick what you know you will be using in the near future. These herbs are gifts from nature, and you should respond accordingly by offering a prayer of thanks whenever you forage. If you respect the land you're foraging from, it will continue to grow what you need. Patience is key.

### Growing Your Own

The middle ground option is growing your own herbs. While these won't have the absolutely unencumbered connection to nature, they are still more connected than store-bought, and your intention in growing them will manifest. If you don't have a yard or garden area, there are many herbs that you can grow yourself just on the windowsill. This might include a learning curve if you're not used to growing things, but it will be well worth it to acclimate yourself to the process and grow closer and more comfortable with nature.

Another benefit to growing herbs yourself is easy and immediate access. You can avoid being caught off guard with a sudden change in your life or the desire to do a particular spell without the tools you need. If you sense a sudden influx of negative energy, you don't need to spend time going to the store or ordering online before you're able to cleanse and purify. You can also seek out other Hoodoo practitioners who grow their own herbs and form relationships with them.

### Harvesting Tips

Harvesting your herbs right after the morning dew has dried is the perfect way to ensure that they have the most oils. This is what keeps them fragrant and what is used in essential oils. With some herbs, you can simply pull the leaves off of the stem. However, with others, you'll want to snip the stem entirely. Make sure you're not too rough with the leaves themselves and, if they're not giving, don't force it.

If you're harvesting flowers, pick them only when they're fully bloomed. Research how that particular plant blooms in your area and keep an eye out for signs of maturation. Since flowers are incredibly delicate, make sure not to handle them more than necessary.

If you're harvesting bark, there are several things to keep in mind in order to respect nature and make sure you get the best yield. Overharvesting bark can be harmful to a tree, so make sure to spread out your harvesting and do research about the health and growth of different trees. Check for things like insects, moss, or signs of disease and wash this off.

If you're looking for roots, harvest after the plant has already died and withered. You can often get the best yield in the fall. Be gentle when harvesting your roots, and make sure not to cut or bruise them. You want to pull the entire root in one piece if possible.

### *Drying and Preserving Herbs*

Once you've harvested and gently washed your herbs, it's time to preserve them so that they remain potent over time. There are many different ways you can go about this, all depending on what you're trying to preserve and your own tools and lifestyle.

### ▸ Air Drying

Keep your herbs separated by type and tie the bundles of herbs together with string or twine. Make sure to date and name them to avoid confusion, then hang them up in a warm place with good circulation, out of direct sunlight to prevent them from getting too dried out. An attic or garage can be a great place to dry your herbs. Once they have a crisp, papery texture, after about 2-3 weeks depending on the herb, your drying process is complete.

If you're trying to collect seeds from these plants, place a bag over the bundle while it dries and the seeds will fall into the bag. If you have smaller herbs or leaves that you need to dry or if you're in a hurry, you can dry your herbs on a cookie sheet or other baking tray instead of hanging them up.

### ▸ Heat Drying

If you're drying your herbs in the oven, you'll need to make sure it's on low heat so you don't cook your herbs. Shoot for 90-110 degrees. You can also leave your oven door slightly open to ensure it doesn't overheat. Move and flip your herbs as necessary and let them dry for about 3-4 hours. You can also use a kitchen dehydrator and follow the instructions.

Heat drying is also best for roots. Cut them into pieces and bake them at 120-140 degrees, flipping throughout. Once they feel light, like sawdust, they're done.

While there are risks of scorching or cooking your herbs, you can use a microwave if you're in a pinch. Make sure they're absolutely dry first, then place your herbs between two pieces of paper towels. Microwave them for 30 seconds at a time until they're dried.

▸ **Storing Your Herbs**

Glass or ceramic jars are the best options, as they are airtight and, if they're opaque, can keep out the light. Date and label your herb jars and keep them in a cool, dark place. Moisture, excess oxygen, and high heat should all be avoided as they can spoil your herbs.

## BEGINNER'S HERB GUIDE

This list of herbs that you can use in your practice is in no way exhaustive. There are also plenty of non-plant items like crystals, stones, and bones that have spiritual properties that can be used in your rituals. As you continue on your journey, you will discover more and more ingredients and come to develop your very own repertoire of go-to herbs. This short-list is to get you started with some of the most commonly used and most valuable herbs so you have somewhere to start.

- **Alfalfa**

Alfalfa is a legume with small purple flowers that grows in warm, temperate climates. Alfalfa is used in money spells and rituals and to avoid hunger and poverty. Just placing a few sprigs in your pocket will help you attract money and prosperity. You can also use the burnt ashes in an amulet.

- **Garlic**

Garlic has a long history of being used in various magical practices. It has a connection with the world of spirits and can be used to grant protection for negative energy, spirits, curses, and the evil eye. It is also associated with willpower.

- **Angelica Root**

This is an edible plant, sometimes referred to as wild celery, though it does appear similar to other poisonous plants. Angelica root provides protection. It wards off negative energy and attracts positive energy. It is also associated with femininity and can be used by women to protect their divine feminine energy. It can be used for healing, purification, removing curses, and counteracting weakness and fatigue.

- **Black Mustard Seed**

Black mustard is a yellow flowering plant and its seeds are either black or brown. It is associated with confusion, conflict, and strife. If you're looking to stir up the mind of your enemy, black mustard seed can do the trick. You can do this by spreading black mustard seed on a place your enemy is known to walk.

- **Chamomile**

In its natural form, chamomile is a flower with white petals and a yellow center that treats a variety of medical issues. Chamomile can promote love and peace while reducing stress. You can use chamomile to benefit your meditation or sleep. It can also be used to increase your luck and prosperity or neutralize any spells or curses that might be put on you.

- **Dandelion Root**

Dandelion will help you connect with spirits and ancestors, which can be incredibly helpful if you find yourself under spiritual attack or if you feel disconnected from the spiritual realm. Use the dandelion root in your divination and to enhance your wishes and prayers.

- **Fennel**

Fennel grows from a white bulb with green stalks and yellow flowers, though the seeds are the most commonly used. It is associated with strength, virility, protection, and healing. Fennel can help you maintain a safe home if you hang it up in your windows. If you ever need a boost to your strength and confidence, turn to fennel.

- **Ginger**

Ginger root is indigenous to China, India, and Hawaii. As it is a tropical plant, it can be difficult to grow outside in the U.S., though you do it in an indoor pot. If you've ever chewed a mouthful of raw ginger, then you have a pretty good idea of what it has to offer. Ginger is sexual, sensual, and has an amplifying and energizing quality. It can attract success and increase a person's desire.

- **Hibiscus**

Hibiscus is a big, gorgeous flower that grows in several different colors. It attracts spirits and is thus helpful in divination, worship, and communication. It's also associated with love and can be used in spells and rituals relating to relationships and marriages.

- **Lemongrass**

Lemongrass looks a lot like chives and grows in bunches of thin, green stalks. This can be used to ward off curses or protect you if you've been jinxed. They also have purifying properties and can be used in cleansing baths.

- **Mandrake Root**

The mandrake root has thick, green leaves and bell-shaped flowers. The root of this plant often has an uncannily human appearance. For this reason, it can be used as a Hoodoo doll, specifically for love purposes. They are related to health, fertility, and protection.

- **Apple Blossoms**

Apple trees yield light pink flowers, and these can be used in divination and are related to love. Apples have historically been associated with fertility, abundance, immortality, and feminine energy.

- **Basil**

Basil is another herb associated with femininity, as it has been used to treat menstrual cramps. It is also used in spells and rituals related to love and relationships. It can be used in marriages to detect if a partner has been unfaithful. Just place a fresh basil leaf in their hand and, if it wilts, this indicates infidelity. It also helps fight against confusion and spiritual tracks and provides protection. Basil can also help you attract success, wealth, and prosperity.

- **Bamboo**

While bamboo is not native to the U.S., it can be grown inside. There are many uses for bamboo. It can be used as a wand, as a vessel to seal spell components, or as materials for spiritual tools. You can also carve a wish into a stalk of bamboo and bury it so that it comes true. Bamboo is also associated with luck and protection.

- **Buckeye**

Buckeyes are a toxic, hard-shelled nut that falls from a few species of tree and shrub in North America, named as such because they resemble a deer's eyeball. They begin to fall usually in August and have usually completely fallen within a month. They've been associated with money and luck and thus are often used to enhance one's odds in gambling. You can do this just by carrying one in your pocket wrapped in a dollar bill or by rubbing a buckeye before you roll dice.

- **Belladonna**

Also known as Deadly Nightshade, this plant has dark green leaves and black berries. It is incredibly poisonous, with the root being the most dangerous part, so it's recommended that inexperienced foragers and rootworkers avoid working with this plant. If you place Belladonna in a secret part of your house, it can provide protection. It can also enhance your communication and worship of your deities and ancestors.

- **Catnip**

Catnip is a common weed that is related and looks very similar to the mint plant. It's associated not only with cats but with the Egyptian lioness goddess Bastet, or Bast, so it can be incredibly useful if you're working with Egyptian pantheons. It's related to beauty, happiness, and love and can also attract helpful spirits.

- **Clover**

There are two types of clover: red and white. This refers to the color of the flower that blooms from them. Both are associated with luck, success, faithfulness, and money. White clover can be used to get rid of evil spirits, while red clover can be used in protection and blessing rituals related to pets.

- **Comfrey**

Comfrey grows in bushes with bell-shaped leaves that can grow in many colors. It's also relatively easy to grow in most environments and has been used medicinally for healing open wounds and treating lung disorders. Comfrey can protect you during travel and provide stability, security, and enhanced endurance. It can also be used in divination and to give you better sleep. Comfrey is toxic to cats and tends to attract cats' attention because it is fragrant, so keep it in places your kitty can't reach.

- **Mugwort**

Mugwort grows in tall, leafy stalks and has a long history of medicinal uses. Specifically, it can be used to delay menstruation and cause miscarriages. Mugwort can protect you against spiritual attacks, ease troubled dreams, and invite prophetic dreams. You can use it in spells relating to sexuality and fertility. It can also enhance your divination and be used in scrying.

- **Yarrow**

Yarrow grows bunches of flowers that can come in a multitude of colors on a thin, green stalk. It's been used to treat wounds and lower fevers. Yarrow is heavily associated with love and can be used to benefit marriage and ensure long-lasting passions, as it protects from negative influences entering the relationship. It not only draws love but enhances self-esteem and courage. It can be harmful if ingested by a pregnant woman or if a person has undiagnosed bleeding.

- **Tobacco**

A lot of tobacco's negative connotation comes from the chemical additives in commercial smoking tobacco. However, it has many positive effects, both medicinally and magically. Historically, it has been used as an antiseptic and to treat hemorrhoids and hernias. It promotes peace and enhances one's personal strength and confidence. It can also help open up communications with spirits and ward off negative energy. You'll want to use natural tobacco and, if you do smoke, try not to use the same tobacco you smoke in your magic.

- **Sandalwood**

Sandalwood is not a singular plant but an entire class of trees used not just for their wood but for their essential oil as well. You can also find it in the form of woodchips or sawdust powder. It's associated with protection and healing and can be used in exorcisms. You can write a wish on a piece of sandalwood and burn it to make that wish come true. You can also scatter sandalwood powder to cleanse the area of negativity.

## MAKING A PROTECTIVE HERB BUNDLE

A protective herb bundle is a simple and easy way to start incorporating rootwork into your life. Herb bundles attract positive and helpful spirits into your house while repelling negative energy, bad luck, and curses. This will allow you to control your spiritual space and positively influence your life. Simply tie a bundle of whole sprigs of the appropriate herbs with a ribbon.

- **Sage**

Sage is used for purification and cleansing in many magical and religious practices. It can bring about wisdom and health. Consider placing this where you work or study to stimulate your thinking and balance out stress.

- **Hyssop**

Hyssop is good for warding off negativity and defending against magic. You can place this around your property if you feel you might be under some sort of spiritual attack, curse, or jinx.

- **Lavender**

A lavender bundle can help attract love into your life, as well as bring peace and calming dreams, making it perfect for hanging up in and around your bed and bedroom. You can also include lavender in a purification bath or ritual.

- **Patchouli**

Patchouli can help repel hostile forces and spirits and can be used similarly to hyssop to protect your home and property.

- **Peppermint**

Peppermint bundles are often used to ward off the 'evil eye,' which refers to the curse or bad luck brought about by being the subject of envy. Place this at your front door if you feel people are watching you with evil intention.

- **Rosemary**

Rosemary is used in many religious ceremonies and has historically been believed to ward off witches. It dispels and protects from negative energy and also assists in meditation. Place it around your property to protect yourself, or place it near your altar to enhance your prayers.

## HERB GARLANDS

By combining several herb bundles into a garland, you can not only decorate your home with beautiful herbs but also boost the intentions of your spells. Hang the individual bundles of herbs on a garland frame or on a string of wire using ribbon and hot glue. You can also add other magical items or charms. Here are a few herbs you can combine to help you get what you want.

- **Healing**

apple blossoms, barley, allspice leaves, eucalyptus, rosemary, sandalwood, wintergreen, lady's mantle, adder's tongue, African violets, cinnamon sticks, dandelion leaf, feverfew

- **Protection**

aloe vera, onion, sandalwood, snapdragon, mugwort, valerian, garlic, dill, mistletoe, gardenia, heather, ivy, lady slipper, mandrake, holly, fleabane, betony, hyssop

- **Love**

catnip, periwinkle, yarrow, daffodil, basil, fig, lavender, apple blossom, bleeding heart, valerian, leek, licorice, magnolia, orange blossoms, rosebuds, saffron, tulip, marjoram

- **Prosperity**

clover, chamomile, buckeye, sunflower, mint, vervain, alfalfa, myrtle, basil, tonka bean, laurel, bergamot, citronella, juniper, nutmeg

## QUICK AND EASY WAYS TO USE HERBS

You can reap the benefits of herbs physically, mentally, and spiritually without the need for complex rituals. Using simple herbs in your rituals is also an easy way to enhance the results. Simply incorporating rootwork into your everyday life will help you tap into your own power and get more accustomed to the power and nuances of herbs as you grow as a practitioner.

### Business, Employment, and Wealth

- **Frankincense**

Carry a piece of frankincense resin with you while you seek employment or go on job interviews to increase your chances of success.

- **Sandalwood**

Write out your professional goals on a piece of sandalwood and burn it in a brazier or incense burner. Pray that you'll get your goal as the smoke carries your wish up into the sky.

- **Laurel/Bay Leaf**

Write your goals on a bay leaf and carry it with you while working towards a promotion or a new job.

- **Basil**

Having a basil plant thriving nearby will give you the courage you need to face challenges in your career.

- **Clover**

Keep clover leaves in your wallet to attract wealth. You can also sprinkle it around your property for the same effect.

- **Chamomile**

Brew some fresh chamomile tea and sprinkle it around your property to attract wealth.

- **Tonka Bean**

Tonka beans are used in many different magical and spiritual practices to attract wealth. Keep one in your pocket or wallet.

- **Pecan**

Baking a pecan pie for yourself can help you build the confidence and courage that you need. If baking isn't your thing, keep a pecan in your pocket during job interviews.

- **Bergamot**

Rub your money with bergamot leaves, then carry a few with you in your wallet. This will help you attract a better-paying job and will make sure all the money you spend comes back to you twofold.

- **Hawthorn Leaf**

Put hawthorn leaves around your workspace to give yourself a masculine boost of confidence and courage in your career.

- **Peppermint**

Wash your hands with peppermint soap or use a prosperity oil with peppermint in it to attract wealth and success. You can also place peppermint above the door of your business to attract customers.

## Luck and Good Fortune

- **Sunflower**

Sunflowers around your property will not only brighten your world but attract good luck to your household. Pick a sunflower as the sun sets and wear it the next day to take that good luck with you.

- **Hazelnut**

Hang a hazelnut branch above your door or carry hazelnuts in your pockets to bring yourself good luck.

- **Holly**

Decorate your home with holly garlands to bring good luck to your household.

- **Pomegranate**

Include pomegranate seeds in your food and drinks to attract good fortune.

- **Snakeroot/ Black Cohosh**

If you feel you've been struck with a string of bad luck or that you've been the target of a curse, place it around your house to neutralize these hostile forces.

- **Chamomile**

To boost your chances of winning at a game or gamble, use chamomile tea to wash your hands right before you play.

- **Buckeye**

Carry a buckeye with you or eat buckeye candies before you gamble to ensure success.

- **Clover/Shamrock**

Place a clover in your pocket or your wallet to attract good luck.

*Legal Troubles*

- **High John the Conqueror Root**

Keep a few pieces of High John the Conqueror root in your pocket during a court hearing to get favorable results.

- **Ginger**

Before you go in for a ruling, chew some raw ginger in your mouth and (discreetly) spit some onto the floor so you can receive a fair judgment.

- **Chamomile**

Take a chamomile bath before court to attract an outcome in your favor.

*Mental Health*

- **Valerian Root**

Drink valerian root tea to relieve anxiety.

- **Dandelion**

While addressing your depression in a spell or ritual, burn dandelion heads on your altar to enhance the results.

- **Honeysuckle**

Eating honeysuckle will give you the inner strength and willpower to continue your battle against depression.

- **Lavender**

Fresh lavender, lavender oil, or lavender incense can be used to relieve headaches and calm nervousness and anxiety. You can also place lavender leaves under your pillow to improve your sleep and relieve stress.

- **Mugwort**

Take a mugwort bath to improve overactive or disturbing dreams.

- **Rosemary**

Keep rosemary close to your bed and use it in any spells or rituals related to sleep to enhance your results.

- **Thyme**

Use thyme in your spells and rituals related to sleep to enhance your results.

*Health and Beauty*

- **Catnip**

Rub whole catnip leaves on your face as a refreshing toner. You can also burn fresh catnip or catnip incense while doing spells and rituals related to beauty to enhance your results.

- **Ginseng**

Use ginseng in your spells and rituals to enhance your beauty and attract the attention of men.

- **Apple Blossoms**

Infuse apple blossoms into vinegar. Rub this infusion on bites or stings to relieve itching and pain.

- **Comfrey**

Use pulverized comfrey leaf juice to heal minor wounds. Drinking comfrey tea can also benefit your overall health.

- **Witch Hazel**

Use witch hazel toner or place whole witch hazel leaves on your skin after cleaning to help tighten pores and dry up excess oils. You can also burn witch hazel leaves or incense in your spells and rituals to help reveal your beauty to others.

- **Rosemary**

Use rosemary to wash your face or after cleaning to give you a brighter complexion and calm breakouts.

- **Eucalyptus**

Burn eucalyptus oil or heat or boil eucalyptus leaves and inhale the vapors to clear out congestion and soothe respiratory issues.

- **Chamomile**

Drink chamomile tea to soothe gastrointestinal distress like constipation, nausea, morning sickness, or stomach aches.

- **Sandalwood**

Add rose or camphor oil into powdered sandalwood and use this as an exfoliant on your skin.

- **Goldenseal**

Rub goldenseal leaves on minor wounds to speed up the healing process.

- **Parthenium**

Boil parthenium leaves down in water and sweeten it with honey or sugar. Drink this mixture for respiratory issues. To relieve itching and pain, you can also use parthenium tincture or ointment on bites or stings.

- **Peppermint**

Freshen your skin with peppermint leaves or chew them to freshen up your breath and teeth. You can also burn peppermint incense or leaves to enhance your rituals and spells related to healing.

## Relationships

- **Violet/Daisy/Daffodil**

Make a garland or carry these flowers with you to attract a lover.

- **Periwinkle**

Place periwinkles in your poppets related to love to enhance the effects.

- **Orange/Lemon**

Make potpourri out of lemon and orange peels and keep them nearby to strengthen your friendships.

- **Vanilla**

Burn vanilla beans or incense when doing rituals or spells related to love and friendship to enhance the results.

- **Sweet Annie**

If you're looking to repair a broken bond, burn sweet Annie herbs or incense in your spells and rituals.

- **Bleeding Heart**

Bleeding heart plants around your property will help attract love into your home.

- **Apple Blossoms**

Burn apple blossom incense or leaves, make an apple blossom potpourri, or drink apple blossom tea to enhance love-related spells or rituals.

- **Tulip**

To attract the person you want and grab their attention, wear a tulip on your body when you're near them.

- **Lavender**

Hang lavender around your home or carry it with you to bring love into your life.

- **Yohimbe**

Take Yohimbe tincture or use Yohimbe in your spells and rituals to deal with impotence and attract more sexual attention.

- **Dill**

Before spending time with the person you want, take a bath with dill seeds to make yourself more attractive to them.

- **Vanilla**

Dab vanilla oil behind your ears and on your pulse points to make you more attractive.

- **Ginseng**

Take a ginseng tincture or tea to enhance your sexual performance.

- **Allspice/Cinnamon/Cloves**

Add this mixture into a cake and give it to the person you want to attract to you.

*Spirituality*

- **Rowan**

Make a divining staff with rowan tree wood. You can also use rowan tree berries and leaves to make an amulet that will strengthen your psychic and spiritual abilities.

- **Mugwort**

Place mugwort in your pillow to attract prophetic dreams.

- **Jasmine**

Placing jasmine in your pillow will bring you prophetic dreams and enhance your decision-making skills and intuition when you're at a crossroads in your life.

- **Heliotrope**

Use heliotrope in your spells and rituals related to prophesy and divination. This can also be used to invoke deities and spirits connected to the sun.

- **Sage**

Use sage in your spells and rituals related to divination to enhance your results.

- **Tobacco Leaf**

Use tobacco leaf in your spells and rituals related to divination to enhance your results.

*Strength*

- **Holly/Mistletoe**

Hang holly or mistletoe around your property or in your doors and windows to protect your home.

- **Heather**

Place heather in your pillow to protect yourself from a magical attack.

- **Mugwort**

Place mugwort in your pillow to protect from magic and psychic attacks and curses. You can also use mugwort in protection oil to enhance the results.

- **Aloe Vera**

Protect yourself from common household slips, falls, and accidents by keeping potted aloe vera around your home.

- **Violet, Honeysuckle, Thistle and Fennel**

Plant, harvest, dry, and hang these herbs around your property to protect yourself and your home. You can also use these herbs to make a protective bag or incense.

- **Hyssop**

Scatter hyssop around your property or carry it with you to provide magical protection.

- **Asafoetida**

Burn asafoetida incense in your spells and rituals related to protection to enhance your results.

- **Mandrake**

Put mandrake leaves under your front door or plant them around your property to provide protection. You can also include it in protection Hoodoo dolls.

- **Oak and Acorns**

An oak tree on your property will grant you strength. You can also carry an acorn in your pocket to tap into your personal power.

- **Laurel/Bay Leaf**

A laurel leaf in your shoe will help you walk with strength and confidence.

- **Cedar**

To enhance your courage in the face of new challenges, carry a few pieces of cedarwood in your pocket.

- **Mullein**

Burn mullein incense or include it in protection bags or potpourri when you're taking on a new task that requires courage.

- **Cinnamon**

Carry a bundle of cinnamon sticks with you or place them under your bed to help enhance your courage.

- **Tonka Bean**

Carry a tonka bean with you to enhance your confidence, specifically in legal matters.

- **Thistle**

Burn thistle herb or incense in your rituals and spells related to your emotional, mental, and spiritual strength. You can also include thistle in a talisman, amulet, or charm related to strength to enhance your results.

## HERBS TO AVOID

Many herbs that are safe to handle or burn as incense can be incredibly dangerous if ingested or rubbed on the skin. They can also be toxic to pets or people with certain conditions. Make sure you do your research before handling a new herb, especially before going out foraging. Do not ingest anything you aren't entirely familiar with. It would be best if you also got comfortable with the scientific names for herbs, as many have both a scientific and folkloric name and this can lead to confusion.

This is far from an exhaustive list, but these are some of the most common toxic herbs you might encounter at the beginning of your practice.

- **Angelica Root**

Angelica root can cause uterine contractions which might cause miscarriage or other complications in pregnant women.

- **Mistletoe**

Mistletoe berries can cause gastrointestinal distress in both humans and animals, though it is far more deadly to cats and dogs. Symptoms include vomiting, nausea, drooling, and stomach pain. Mistletoe leaves can also cause miscarriages in pregnant women.

- **Peppermint Oil**

Peppermint essential oil can cause liver damage and failure, respiratory distress in infants, and can trigger uterine contractions, which may cause miscarriage in pregnant women and animals.

- **Tobacco**

Tobacco leaves can be harmful and even fatal for animals, specifically dogs and cats. Symptoms include vomiting, elevated and abnormal heart rate, and paralysis.

- **Goldenseal**

Goldenseal can be dangerous to infants and breastfeeding women and can also cause miscarriage in pregnant women.

- **Jimson Grass**

This common weed is incredibly poisonous to animals of all sizes if ingested, from cats to horses and, of course, humans. Symptoms include anxiety, dilated pupils, restlessness, and hallucinations before death.

- **Mugwort**

Mugwort has long since been used to cause miscarriages and should be avoided by pregnant women. It is also a common allergen and might cause sneezing, coughing, and itching.

- **Holly Berries**

Holly berries are toxic and possibly fatal to humans and most pets. Symptoms include vomiting, diarrhea, drowsiness, head shaking, and dehydration.

- **Basil**

Basil can induce uterine contractions, which may speed up menstruation or raise the risk of miscarriage in pregnant women.

- **Pennyroyal**

Pennyroyal herb can cause uterine contractions that speed up menstruation or cause miscarriage in pregnant women. However, pennyroyal oil is far more toxic and can be fatal. Symptoms include nausea, vomiting, abdominal pain, bleeding, seizures, and organ failure.

- **Rosemary**

Rosemary can speed up menstruation or cause miscarriage in pregnant women. It can also be toxic in very high doses and may cause vomiting, spasms, and fluid buildup in the lungs. Rosemary can also be dangerous to people with high blood pressure, Crohn's disease, or ulcerative colitis.

- **Yarrow**

Yarrow can speed up menstruation and might raise the risk of miscarriage in pregnant women. It can also be dangerous to those with blood disorders as it may slow blood clotting.

- **Black Cohosh**

Black cohosh can speed up menstruation and cause miscarriage in pregnant women. It can also cause mild side effects like gastrointestinal distress, headache, or rash and may be dangerous for those with liver disease, seizures, and a high risk of stroke or blood clots.

- **Comfrey**

Comfrey can cause liver damage, especially to pregnant mothers and fetuses, if ingested or absorbed through the skin in high amounts.

- **Parthenium**

Parthenium is a common allergen and can cause sneezing, coughing, and running nose. It's also used to speed up menstruation and may be dangerous to fetuses.

- **Catnip**

Catnip can speed up menstruation and cause miscarriage in pregnant women. It can also cause an upset stomach and nausea if ingested in high doses.

- **Buckeye**

Buckeye nuts that have not been appropriately prepared by boiling, peeling, and soaking to remove the toxic chemical are dangerous and possibly fatal to pets and humans. Symptoms include vomiting, diarrhea, convulsions, weakness, and paralysis.

- **Chamomile**

Chamomile can be dangerous to pets, especially if they already have an allergy to a plant in the ragweed family. Symptoms include vomiting, diarrhea, and skin irritation.

## CONCLUSION

With time, practice, and wisdom, you can develop your rootwork abilities to the point of being able to offer healing not only to yourself but others. However, it's important not to fly too close to the sun when you first begin. You don't want to risk getting burnt out or discouraged by mistakes. There is also a lot of danger when you start working with wild plants or making healing waters or potions.

# 5

# SPELLCASTING

Spells are often depicted in popular media as wild and dangerous acts of the supernatural. However, in truth, a spell is a ritual that aligns your intentions and spiritual strength in order to help your desires come true. Intention, once again, is vital, as spells won't work if you are not focused and aware of what you truly want and what your goal is. By performing a series of actions that focus your mind and energy while also giving thanks to the spirits and deities who assist you with your own spiritual power, you can affect the world around you. Spells represent your faith in both the spiritual and in yourself.

While some witchcraft practices include group or collective spells, in Hoodoo, spells are done in a solitary environment. This makes Hoodoo spellcasting extremely personal. The exact ingredients, the amount used of each ingredient, and the specifics of how you complete the ritual can be different for each person. Hoodoo spells can include many objects, including oils, candles, herbs, the Bible, powders, cloth, crystals, and more. What we're going over are the basics of spellcasting that you need to adhere to in order to ensure you get what you truly want.

## PREPARING TO CAST A SPELL

You might not always have the opportunity to fully prepare each time you have a spell and this is ok, as you can modify a spell for specific scenarios. However, there are a few steps you can take that will enhance the efficacy of your spells.

### *Creating an Altar*

While ancestral altars will help you utilize the wisdom and powers of your spirits, deities, and ancestors in your spellcasting, you can also create an altar specifically for the spell you want to cast. When creating a ritual-specific altar, you can use a regular table or simply a cloth on the floor—whatever works for you as long as it is large enough to place several related items on it. This should be treated similarly to your ancestral altar, as every item should be cleansed and purified.

On top of the specific items needed for each particular spell, you can add items that you feel may make your spell more powerful. Keep color in mind, as different types of spells are associated with different colors, as we will discuss. For example, if you're doing a love spell on a particular person, you could include red cloths, rose quartz, an item belonging to that person, etc.

### Ritual Baths

We encounter and absorb many different energies throughout the day. Just as we bathe to wash away the filth of living a whole life, we must spiritually cleanse ourselves to wash away negative energies that might affect our ability to practice. Ritual purification baths can do many things to help you maintain positive energy that will not interfere and will actually enhance your magical abilities. They also allow you to come before your ancestors clean and pure in order to show respect for them.

They help you open yourself up to the spiritual. They can assist in severing unhealthy ties that might disrupt our spiritual abilities. These ties could be romantic, mental, or generational curses. Anything that binds you to something negative is a tie that needs to be severed for you to reach your full potential. Ritual baths can also make you more attractive to the things you want in your life and can help protect you from harmful forces.

You can also perform an internal cleanse by ingesting a specific mixture of herbs in order to clear your mind and purge negativity from your body. However, this practice is not without its risks. Many herbs used in Hoodoo are poisonous when ingested, and a beginner can easily hurt themselves by attempting an internal cleanse. This is a practice best saved for more experienced practitioners.

While the specifics of your purification bath can vary, I will provide a basic bath ritual that you can perform either once a month or once a quarter, depending on your needs. This is a three-day ritual meant to entirely cleanse you so that you can work at your most powerful. The first bath should be done just after sunset and is intended to repel negative energies. The second bath is done just after dawn and attracts positive energy. The final bath is meant to reinforce this positive energy and seal in your intentions. If you experience a menstrual cycle, do not do this bath while bleeding, as blood is magically powerful and will interfere with the process.

- **Day One**

*You'll need*: dandelion roots, yarrow, wormwood, nettle, flower petals that are red or purple, horehound, ½ cup of vinegar, and a few drops of ammonia.

*Step One*: Fill your bathtub as hot as is comfortable.

*Step Two*: Place two candles on opposite ends of the bath as a doorway and light them.

*Step Three*: Pour your herbs, ammonia, and vinegar into the water.

*Step Four*: Take off your clothes and step through the doorway into the water.

*Step Five*: Immerse yourself in the water and think about the hostile forces in your life.

*Step Six*: Dunk yourself in the water seven times and, each time you resurface, spend a few minutes thinking about the positive things you want in your life. Detach yourself from the negative things that are causing you emotional and spiritual distress.

*Step Seven*: Step out of the bathtub through the doorway. Do not dry yourself.

*Step Eight*: Scoop out a cup of the bathwater and set it aside while the rest drains.

*Step Nine*: Once you've air-dried, put on a robe and take the cup outside. Face the west and hold the cup over your head while you recite these words: "Whatever holds the negative forces or spirits have over me has been broken. I am free from every negative bond. As I cast this water over my head, I am also casting out every spirit and energy in my life" (Belard, 2020).

*Step Ten*: Toss the water.

- **Day Two**

*You'll need*: angelica root, chamomile, hyssop, allspice, comfrey leaves, powdered nutmeg, powdered cinnamon, white flower petals, honey, 3 cups of milk, and one egg.

*Step One*: Take a private bath and get as clean as possible. Make sure your bathtub is also clean.

*Step Two*: Fill your bathtub as hot as is comfortable.

*Step Three*: Place two candles on opposite ends of the bath as a doorway and light them.

*Step Four*: Crack the egg into the water.

*Step Five*: Add your herbs, petals, and spices into the water.

*Step Six*: Pour your milk and honey into the water.

*Step Seven*: Step into the bathtub through the doorway and immerse yourself. Allow yourself to enjoy the sweet aroma.

*Step Eight*: Dunk yourself into the water five times. Each time you resurface, open yourself to the positive energy surrounding you.

*Step Nine*: Step out of the tub through the doorway. Do not dry yourself.

*Step Ten*: Scoop a cup of the water out and allow the rest to drain.

*Step Eleven*: Once you've air-dried, put on a robe and take the cup outside. Face the east, hold the cup close to your chest, and recite these words: "I welcome this day with joy and gladness. I open myself to the blessing that the world has to offer me. I attract light, love, and positivity in every area of my life. I welcome all the good spirits into my heart and into my home"(Belard, 2020).

*Step Twelve*: Toss the water towards the rising sun.

*Step Thirteen*: Allow yourself time to soak in the positive energy around you before you wash yourself off.

- **Day Three**

Day three is a repeat of day two. Make sure to use entirely new and fresh herbs.

### *Meditate and Define Your Intentions*

We as humans have an incredible ability to lie to ourselves or obscure truths and hide them away in our subconscious. Meditation and being clear on your intentions are essential in making sure you truly know what you want. If you are trying to hide insecurity, uncertainty, or doubt, this can seriously affect the efficacy of your spellcasting.

Try writing out your intentions on a piece of paper. Let your thoughts flow and allow yourself to be honest. Your spellcasting area is your space, and you should release yourself from fear of judgment. Be as specific as you possibly can be.

While Hoodoo does allow vengeance in the sense of an eye for an eye, you must still have good intentions and the goal to increase the happiness of yourself and others through your magic.

You can also try more traditional meditation techniques, such as mindfulness or yoga, to center your thoughts and clear your head of negativity and distractions. Use this time to communicate with, praise, worship, and seek guidance from your ancestors, spirits, and deities. While Hoodoo is a solitary practice, it is not a lonely one.

You also express your intentions through your prayers. Most of the spells we are going to discuss include some ritual words. These words are borrowed from long and rich Hoodoo traditions, most of which are Christian but not all. Your prayers can and should be specific to your religious beliefs, the deities you work with, and your ancestors.

## TYPES OF SPELLS

Spells can be organized in several different ways, such as by the tools used or the ritual method. The broadest organization is by color. These are the three most common color types for spells, and while this doesn't cover every kind of spell you could be casting, it's a great starting point.

## White Magic

White magic spells are pure and geared towards happiness and harmony. These spells help resolve problems, eliminate negativity and bad influences, and bring peace.

### ▶ Attract Money

You'll need the following ingredients: a green ritual candle, something you can use to engrave your candle, water, a bowl, and seven-star anise seeds.

*Step One*: Engrave three words into your green candle: Chrimata, Dirua, Maritupe.

*Step Two*: Pour your water into your bowl.

*Step Three*: Light your green candle.

*Step Four*: Throw your anise seeds into the water one at a time. Each time you do, recite these magic words: "Saau ia ia te au chrimata. Sau ia ia te au dirua. Sau ia ia te au maritupe. By the virtue of this seed, I will prosper. Para chrimata. Para dirua. Para maritupe. A little richer, I shall be. Yes, I do. Yes, I will be a little richer"(Williamson, 2021).

*Step Five*: Let the candle melt entirely and leave the anise seeds in your water.

*Step Six*: After seven days, take the anise seeds out of the water and carry them around in your wallet.

▶ **Candle Spell for Wealth**

You'll need the following ingredients: honey, powdered cinnamon, sugar, a charcoal disc, High John the Conqueror root, a tiger's eye stone, powdered frankincense, a bowl, a spoon, a small towel, and a small green candle.

*Step One*: Put your honey, cinnamon, and sugar into the bowl and mix into a paste.

*Step Two*: Carve the Fehu rune ᚠ into the candle.

*Step Three*: Rub the paste onto the candle from top to bottom.

*Step Four*: Light your incense.

*Step Five*: Light your candle.

*Step Six*: Place some of the paste on your tongue but don't swallow it.

*Step Seven*: Focus on the candle and speak your intentions out loud, including what you want money for and expressing your gratitude.

*Step Eight*: Swallow the paste.

*Step Nine*: Place the High John the Conqueror root and the tiger's eye beside the candle.

*Step Ten*: Let the candle burn out.

*Step Eleven*: Bury the incense ash and the rest of the candle in the ground or in a natural body of water.

### ▸ The Santa Lucia Spell to Win a Game

You'll need the following ingredients: seawater, an unused terracotta vase, seven white candles, and a green silk ribbon.

*Step One*: Pour your seawater into the terracotta vase.

*Step Two*: Place your candles in a circle around the vase.

*Step Three*: Light your candles one by one while reciting these words: "Oh glorious Saint Lucia, who by the light has your name, hear me"(Williamson, 2021).

*Step Four*: Wash your ribbon in the seawater and recite these words three times:

I believe in God, Almighty Father, Creator of heaven and Earth. And in Jesus Christ, His only Son, our Lord, who was conceived of the Holy Spirit was born of the Virgin Mary suffered under Pontius Pilate, was crucified, died, and was buried, he descended into hell: On the third day, he rose from the dead: he ascended to heaven, he sits at the right hand of God the Father Almighty, from there he will come to judge the living and the dead. I believe in the Holy Spirit, the Holy Catholic Church, the communion of saints, the remission of sins, the resurrection of the flesh, eternal life. Amen. (Williamson, 2021)

*Step Five*: Let the candles melt entirely.

*Step Six*: Dry the ribbon in the sun.

*Step Seven*: Carry the green silk ribbon with you when you play the game as an amulet for good luck.

▸ **The Brazilian Spell for Increasing Personal Power**

You'll need the following ingredients: a white candle, coconut milk, an unused sponge, a bathtub, and two tablespoons of saffron.

*Step One*: Light your candle.

*Step Two*: Stare into the flame unblinking and, as you do, repeat these words until you can't hold your eyes open: "Aayan lese wura. Wuru lese aayan"(Williamson, 2021).

*Step Three*: Draw a hot bath and pour your coconut milk and saffron into the water.

*Step Four*: Soak in the bath and use the sponge all over your body while repeating the same words.

▸ **Increase Luck**

You'll need the following ingredients: a clove of garlic, parsley, salt, incense ashes, a small white silk bag, and seven different churches.

*Step One*: Place your garlic, parsley, salt, and incense ashes into your bag.

*Step Two*: Go to a church and dip your bag into the holy water.

*Step Three*: Sit down and recite this version of the Lord's prayer:

Our father who art in heaven, hallowed be thy name, thy kingdom come, thy will be done on earth as it is in heaven, give us this day our daily bread, lead us not into temptation and deliver us from our enemies who want us evil, and deliver me from my enemies who want me evil. Amen (Williamson, 2021).

*Step Four*: Repeat steps two and three for a total of seven churches.

*Step Five*: Carry the bag with you always for good luck.

### ▸ Good Luck Charm

You'll need the following ingredients: High John the Conqueror root, one whole nutmeg, a coin, green cloth, green ribbon, and a small green candle.

*Step One*: Light the candle and allow it to melt down.

*Step Two*: Fix the coin into the soft wax.

*Step Three*: Place the coin in the wax along with the nutmeg and High Conqueror John root on the cloth.

*Step Four*: Tie the cloth closed with the ribbon.

*Step Five*: Carry the charm with you to attract wealth and luck to your finances.

### ▸ Find Peace and Serenity

You'll need the following ingredients: twelve white candles and a full moon.

*Step One*: Light your candles one by one in a circle around you.

*Step Two*: For each candle, recite these words: "Sub tuum praesidium confugimus, sancta Dei Genitrix, nostras deprecationes ne despicias in neccessitatibus, sed a periculis cunctis libera nos semper, Virgo gloriosa et benedicta. Amen" (Williamson, 2021).

*Step Three*: Stay in the circle of light and allow the negativity to leave you.

### ▸ Happiness Potion

You'll need these ingredients: an ampoule or vial with a cap, dried and pulverized dandelion flowers, one tablespoon of oregano powder, one tablespoon of cinnamon powder, one tablespoon of thyme powder, and seven pine needles.

*Step One*: Place all the powders into the ampoule.

*Step Two*: Kneel facing the east and hold the vial in your hands.

*Step Three*: Recite Psalm No. 7 seven times:

Lord, my God, in you I have found refuge: save me from those who persecute me and set me free, so that you do not tear me apart like a lion, tearing me apart without anyone freeing me. Lord, my God, if I have acted in this way, if there is injustice in my hands, if I have repaid my friends with evil, if I have stripped my adversaries for no reason, let the enemies pursue me and join me, trample my life on the ground and cast my honor into dust. Arise, O Lord, in your wrath, rise up against the wrath of my adversaries, be unshaken, my God, make a judgment! The assembly of peoples surrounds you: return from above to dominate it! The Lord judges the people. Judge me, Lord, according to my justice, according to the innocence that is in me. Cease the wickedness of the wicked. Make the righteous firm, you who scrutinize mind and heart, righteous God. My shield is in God: He saves the righteous of heart. God is a righteous judge, God is outraged every day. Does he not return to sharpen his sword, to tend, to point his bow? He prepares instruments of death, rekindles his arrows. Behold, the evil one conceives injustice, is pregnant with wickedness, gives birth to lies. He digs a deep well and falls into the pit he has made: his wickedness falls on his head, his violence falls on his head. I will give thanks to the Lord for his righteousness and sing the name of God, the Most High (Williamson, 2021).

*Step Four*: Keep this ampoule or vial with you for happiness and good luck.

▸ **Prosperity Vase**

You'll need the following ingredients: oil, seven leaves of rosemary, seven bay leaves, seven basil leaves, seven thyme leaves, seven lavender leaves, seven cloves, three silver coins, three green candles, three golden candles, a terracotta jar, and a wooden stick.

*Step One*: Put all of your herbs and the three silver coins into the terracotta jar.

*Step Two*: Cover the contents of your terracotta jar with oil.

*Step Three*: Arrange your candles around the terracotta jar in alternating order—one gold, one green, one gold, etc.

*Step Four*: Light your candles.

*Step Five*: Use the wooden stick to stir the contents of the jar clockwise.

*Step Six*: As you're stirring your jar, recite these words seven times: "Paisa. Panam. Pecunia. Penz. Para. Dirua" (Williamson, 2021).

*Step Seven*: Mix the contents of the jar counterclockwise.

*Step Eight*: As you're stirring your jar, recite these words seven times: "Aurid. Arap. Znep. Manap. Asiap."

*Step Nine*: Break the wooden stick into two pieces and place them in the jar.

*Step Ten*: Let the candles burn out completely.

*Step Eleven*: Store the jar near a doorway or window.

### ▸ Protection From the Evil Eye

You'll need these ingredients: garlic, water, salt, oil, a copper pot, three white candles, and a photo of the person who has cursed you with the evil eye.

*Step One*: Place the white candles around the copper pot and light them one by one.

*Step Two*: As you light each candle, recite these words: "Glory to the Father and the Son and the Holy Spirit. As it was in the beginning, now and always, for ever and ever. Amen" (Williamson, 2021).

*Step Three*: Add water to the copper pot.

*Step Four*: Rub your garlic on the picture of the person who you want to be freed from.

*Step Five*: Chop the garlic and put it in the pot along with your salt and oil.

*Step Six*: Burn the photograph.

*Step Seven*: As the photograph burns, recite these words: "Garlic, salt, and oil. Go away evil eye that I don't want you. Burn the evil eye. Broken is the enchantment. In the name of the Father, the Son, and the Holy Spirit" (Williamson, 2021).

*Step Eight*: Throw a little more salt and oil into the pot.

*Step Nine*: Wait until the next morning, then toss the contents of the water into a stream while reciting three Our Fathers and three Hail Marys.

### ▸ Protection Spell

You won't need any special ingredients for this spell.

*Step One*: Go out to a field at dawn.

*Step Two*: Recite these words three times:

"Pater noster dei sanctorum. Maria bella angelorum. Beautiful Mary sleeping. And the baby Jesus appeared to her in a dream. Dear, I dreamt that at the ordeal they brought you. Golden crowns have lifted you up and thorns have wanted you. What you are saying is truth, the Church answered to your mother. And whoever says this three times in a field is not afraid of water, thunder, or lightning" (Williamson, 2021).

### ▸ Protection Charm

You'll need the following ingredients: 9 white mustard seeds, a nail, a hammer, a red cloth, and a red ribbon.

*Step One*: Place the mustard seeds on the red cloth.

*Step Two*: Tie the cloth closed with the ribbon.

*Step Three*: Nail the bag on the inside of your front door for protection.

### ▸ Ancient Money Attraction Spell

You'll need the following ingredients: a white candle, a chestnut leaf, a silver coin, and a new moon.

*Step One*: Go out, preferably on a Monday night, and light the white candle.

*Step Two*: As you light your candle, recite five Our Fathers and five Hail Marys.

*Step Three*: Wrap the silver coin in the chestnut leaf.

*Step Four*: Recite these words ten times: "Today is the moon, tomorrow is Mars. My fate, my beautiful one don't leave me alone. Come meet me, do not frighten me, let me discover the wealth" (Williamson, 2021).

*Step Five*: Let the candle burn out completely.

*Step Six*: Keep the silver coin wrapped in the chestnut leaf in your wallet.

### ▸ Quick Cash

You'll need the following ingredients: bay leaf, cinnamon powder, nutmeg powder, and a white candle.

*Step One*: Mix a generous amount of your herbs together.

*Step Two*: Light your candle.

*Step Three*: Meditate on your intent and the specific need you are working to fulfill. Say a prayer asking for the money you need.

*Step Four*: Burn the mixture of herbs and fan the smoke towards you, allowing your face and hands to absorb the smoke.

### ▸ Prosperity Water

You'll need the following ingredients: two goldenseal roots, two handfuls of sassafras leaves, two handfuls of marigold petals, a strainer or cheesecloth, and a gallon of regular or holy water.

*Step One*: Boil your herbs in the water.

*Step Two*: Strain the water through a strainer or cheesecloth.

*Step Three*: Pray Psalm 4 as you stir the water clockwise.

*Step Four*: Bury the remaining herbs.

*Step Five*: Use this water in ritual baths as a cleansing liquid in your altar and home, or spritz it around your work area to attract prosperity.

### ▸ Black Salt Powder for Protection

You'll need the following ingredients: black pepper, salt, wood ash, charcoal, a bowl, and a mortar and pestle.

*Step One*: Grind all of your ingredients together in a clockwise motion with your mortar and pestle.

*Step Two*: Once the powder is evenly ground, pour it into a bowl and pray Psalm 91 over it.

*Step Three*: Sprinkle this salt in a circle around anything you wish to protect.

### Red Magic

Red magic spells are associated with love, passion, and attraction. They can be used to make yourself more attractive, to enhance your sexual and romantic life, or increase someone else's feelings for you. However, these spells don't work against the person's will as you can't force someone to have feelings for you. It's better to understand them as creating the circumstances and ambiance that make love and passion more likely to bloom.

Love spells come with their own unique challenges. It's crucial to be acutely aware of your own emotions and intentions. Are your feelings for this person genuine? Why do you want this person to have feelings for you? Is it out of genuine love and attraction or out of a negative emotion like spite or jealousy? How does this person feel about you? Do you really want this person in your life? Are they capable of healthily processing the feelings of love and passion in a way that is not destructive to you or them?

### ▸ Make Them Contact You

You'll need the following ingredients: licorice root, a dime or mercury dime, a paper with the person's name written on it, and purple cloth.

*Step One*: Wrap the dime and licorice root up in the paper with the name of the person you want to contact you.

*Step Two*: Wrap all of this in the purple cloth.

*Step Three*: Recite your intentions aloud by saying something like: "I want you to contact me, X."

*Step Four*: Place the wrapped package on the floor and stomp on it.

*Step Five*: Repeat this nine times a day for nine days.

### ▸ Follow Me Boy Oil to Attract Love, Wealth, Luck, and Make Yourself Stand Out

You'll need the following ingredients: angelica root, catnip, coriander seed, damiana, fennel seed, and grapeseed or almond oil.

*Step One*: Mix your herbs together.

*Step Two*: Pour your herbs into the oil.

*Step Three*: Place your mixture in a warm place for several days.

You can use this oil in other spells, such as the Come My Way Orange.

### ▸ Come My Way Orange to Attract Love

You'll need the following ingredients: a whole orange, a rose, nine pins, red thread, a lock of your own hair, Follow Me Boy Oil, and a carving knife.

*Step One*: Anoint your lock of hair, the pins, and thread with the Follow Me Boy Oil.

*Step Two*: Carve a small hole into the orange.

*Step Three*: Insert the rose and your lock of hair into the orange.

*Step Four*: Close the hole in the orange with the pins.

*Step Five*: Weave the red thread through the pins.

*Step Six*: Bury the orange near your property or your phone and wait for contact from love interests to pour in.

### ▸ Make Someone Think About You

You'll need the following ingredients: an unused mirror, a picture of yourself, a picture of the person you'd like to think about you, tape, and a white candle.

*Step One*: Place the picture of the person you want to think about you face down on the mirror's reflective surface.

*Step Two*: Place your own picture face down on the back of the mirror.

*Step Three*: Wrap tape around the mirror to adhere the two photos to the mirror.

*Step Four*: Light your white candle.

*Step Five*: Hold the mirror against your heart and recite these words 49 times: "Every time you see your reflection you will think of me. Thame. Skefteis."

*Step Six*: Let the candle burn out completely.

*Step Seven*: Store the mirror under your bed.

▸ **Attract Love, Friendship, and Good Luck**

You'll need the following ingredients: rosewater, three strawberries, three whole vanilla bean pods, three tablespoons of cocoa powder, three tablespoons of salt, a saucepan, one glass bottle, a cheesecloth or other filter, one sheet of paper, and a red marker.

*Step One*: Pour your rosewater, strawberries, vanilla, cocoa powder, and salt into your saucepan and boil for 30 minutes on low heat.

*Step Two*: Use your red marker to write these words on your sheet of paper: "Pure love. Strong love. Open all the doors to me. Pure love. Strong friendship. Luck be favorable Amen" (Williamson, 2021).

*Step Three*: Roll up the piece of paper and place it in your glass bottle.

*Step Four*: Pour the mixture in your pot through your cheesecloth or filter and into the glass bottle and seal it.

*Step Five*: Hold the bottle in your hands and shake it while reciting the words you wrote on the paper seven times.

*Step Six*: Store the bottle in a dark place.

▸ **Love Spell Using Hair**

You'll need the following ingredients: five hairs from the person you want to fall in love with you, five of your own hairs, a red wool thread, a red candle, a yellow candle, and a green candle.

*Step One*: Place the candles in a triangle on the ground.

*Step Two*: Tie your hairs and the hairs of the person you want to fall for you together with the red string. Place this in the center of the three candles.

*Step Three*: Light the candles one at a time in order of red, green, yellow.

*Step Four*: For each candle, recite these words: "Ure, sanctus spiritus, renes nostros, et or nostrum, domine."

*Step Five*: Let the candle burn out completely.

*Step Six*: Bury the hair near the house of the person you want to fall in love with you.

▸ **Make Yourself Fall in Love**

You'll need the following ingredients: salt, a lock of hair, nine red candles, nine green candles, and nine yellow candles.

*Step One*: Create a large circle of salt on the floor.

*Step Two*: Place the candles around the circle in alternating colors red, green, yellow, red, green, yellow, etc.

*Step Three*: Step inside the circle and light the candles clockwise, starting with the candle that faces the east.

*Step Four*: Hold the lock of hair in your right hand and repeat the name of the person you want to fall in love with 99 times while visualizing the person.

*Step Five*: Let the candles wear out.

*Step Six*: Keep the hair in your pillowcase.

▸ **Love Ligament of Venus**

You'll need the following ingredients: an apple, two squares of paper, one hair from the person you want to fall for you, your own hair, needle and red thread, a wooden box, bay leaves, a red candle, and your own blood.

*Step One*: Using your own blood, write your own name on one square of paper, and the name of the person you want to fall for you on the other.

*Step Two*: Cut the apple in two and remove the seeds.

*Step Three*: Tie your hair and the hair of the person you want to fall for you together.

*Step Four*: Place the two squares of paper and the two hairs inside of the apple.

*Step Five*: Use the red thread to sew the two parts of the apple back together.

*Step Six*: Place the apple into the wooden box and cover it with bay leaves.

*Step Seven*: Close the box and place the red candle on top of it.

*Step Eight*: Light the candle and repeat these words seven times:

Venus mother, immortal Venus, daughter of Jupiter. To you who alone dominate nature and without you nothing is born. I invoke you and I beg you. Let (person's name) quickly come to me. Make her/him/them fall madly in love with me. That he can no longer eat, drive, or sleep except with me. O Venus, glorious goddess, to you whom I said "If he does not love you already, he will soon so so" I address my humble begging. Make him fall in love with me, even against his will. So be it and so it will be.

*Step Nine*: Let the candle burn out completely.

*Step Ten*: Store the box under your bed.

### ▸ Ishtar's Love Ligament

You'll need the following ingredients: a one-meter-long red silk ribbon

*Step One*: At night, tie a knot in the silk ribbon while reciting these words: "In the name of Ishtar, the one who makes everything fruitful, I tie you to me, and your love for me day by day as it on the wall will grow. So it will be."

*Step Two*: Repeat for 48 consecutive nights.

*Step Three*: On the 49ths day, go to a crossroads in the country, burn the ribbon, and scatter the ashes.

### ▸ Marriage

You'll need the following ingredients: red rose petals, rose water, and a pen.

*Step One*: Write your beloved's name on each rose petal.

*Step Two*: Dip each petal into the rosewater.

*Step Three*: Sprinkle the petals outside of your beloved's house.

### ▸ Bring a Lover Back

You'll need the following ingredients: a glass jar, red wine, one red candle, seven pieces of red paper, a black felt tip pen, and scissors.

*Step One*: Cut seven hearts out of the piece of paper.

*Step Two*: On each paper heart, write these words: "(Name of the person you want to come back) cinta saya kembali kepada saya."

*Step Three*: Light the red candle.

*Step Four*: Recite these words seven times: Kerana scheva mencintai saya lagi. Kembali kepada saya. Cinta saya lagi dan lagi."

*Step Five*: Fill your glass jar with red wine.

*Step Six*: Set your paper ears on fire with the candle flame one at a time. As they burn, throw them into the jar while reciting these words: "Kembali kepada saya."

*Step Seven*: Seal the jar so that it is airtight.

*Step Eight*: Let the candle burn out completely.

*Step Nine*: Keep the jar under your bed.

**Black Magic**

Unlike most other Hoodoo spells, black magic allows you to obtain your wishes without paying mind to ethics. Black magic is very powerful and can allow you to curse or harm others or protect yourself from serious curses. However, not only do you have to worry about imbuing yourself with the power to do harm, but it is also very difficult and very dangerous. Black magic casting is far out of the realm of safety for any newcomer to Hoodoo and should be taken very seriously.

## CONCLUSION

These spells will help you get accustomed to the ritual of spellcasting and cover many of the common desires practitioners have. Make sure to treat all of your objects and rituals with respect, dignity, and focus. Most importantly, do not neglect to pay attention to your mind, spiritual energy, and intentions. Even if you follow each spell instruction to the letter, you might not reap the desired outcome of your spell if you are not clear on what you want or if you are reckless with the forces you're working with.

# 6

# CANDLES, OILS, AND BONES

As you may have noticed in the previous chapters, oils and candles play a very important role in spellcasting and understanding how and why in more depth will help you strengthen your spells and enhance the kind of changes you can bring about.

## CANDLES BASICS

Candles are one of the few things that seem to have universal significance in all cultures. Countless rituals relate to candles and their spiritual power. Lighting birthday candles began as a ritual to protect a child from evil spirits, with the ritual being renewed each year to ensure their protection. Many cultures light candles or lanterns to honor the death of a loved one and guide their soul back to the source. There is undeniable power and importance in candles. To be the strongest Hoodoo practitioner you can be, you'll need to know how to harness that strength.

### *Candles' Effect on the Mind*

Candles serve an important purpose in any spiritual practice outside of their magical uses. If you find that your spells are regularly not working or you're getting undesirable results, it may be because your mind is unfocused or cluttered. Thoughtful candle use can help with that. They allow you to focus and elevate your psychic energy and help you get in tune with your own spiritual energy. They also help you to focus, clear your mind, and dispel stress and mental distractions. Focusing your mind and intentions can be incredibly difficult, especially if you're working to deal with a problem that deeply upsets you or if you're neurodivergent and including candles not only in your rituals but in your worship and meditation, even if it's not strictly called for, can be incredibly helpful.

### *The Spiritual Significance of Candles*

The importance of light is referenced over and over again in various religions and in spiritual and magic systems. Light is a sort of pure energy and life force. It is symbolic of the soul or spirit of a thing and illuminates the darkness so the truth can be seen. By exercising control over the physical light around us through the use of candles, lamps, or flashlights, we're able to engage with the metaphysical light of the spiritual realm. The transformative effect of fire on the candle is also very important in the power of candle magic.

## Which Candles to Use

There are a few things to keep in mind when selecting candles to use in your rituals. Firstly, it must be made of natural wax, like beeswax or soy wax. Kerosene wax releases carcinogenic fumes and should be avoided. You should also make sure your candle has a cotton core as opposed to nylon or another synthetic fiber. You want your candle to be pure without added chemicals or fragrances, which can work against the spell you're working.

Your candle should also be in perfect shape without imperfections, cracks, or damage. Use a new candle for each ritual, and make sure to consecrate the candle before using it. You can do this by rubbing it down with a purifying oil or using purifying smoke. Avoid spiritual water as this might wet the wick and make it difficult to light.

The size of your candle is also important. If your spell calls to let your candle burn all the way out, as most do, you don't want a candle that will take three days to burn. Some spells call for specific types of candles, like seven-day candles.

Color is another hugely important factor in candle magic. The importance of color association in magic in general, but specifically Hoodoo, is reflected in candle usage. Different spells call on candles of different colors because of their ability to boost the energy of the spell. You can dive more into the specifics of color by researching color theory and getting familiar with the color wheel, but for now, let's focus on the main color families. You can also find color-based wisdom by studying chakra and crystal healing.

- **Black Candles**

Do not confuse black candles with black magic. Black is considered a neutral color, and while some black magic spells might call for black candles, the use of black candles is not inherently malevolent. Black is associated with protection and dominance and might be called upon if you're trying to assert your will over another person. It can also be used when calling upon demonic spirits or when doing spells related to death and grief.

- **White Candles**

White candles and their glow are considered purifying. They are also associated with protection as well as peace, harmony, and calm. It is a very spiritual but also a neutral color, so it can always be used to improve your clarity and spellcasting.

- **Green Candles**

As you might have guessed, green attracts money. It's also associated with nature, prosperity, fertility, and luck. If you're looking to make some aspect of your life or world grow or become abundant, green candles might be helpful.

- **Yellow Candles**

Yellow is brightening and lifts moods and is associated with the sun. Yellow candles are used in rituals surrounding happiness, friendship, and joy as well as success and recognition. They are helpful if you're finding yourself down or depressed such that it affects your ability to focus on your spells.

- **Silver Candles**

The moon is often considered the divine feminine energy, and silver candles draw upon that femininity. If a spell calls for moonlight, but you're in a rush or can't wait until that specific phase of the moon, you can use silver candles to cast a moon-like glow. Silver candles can also help you get in contact with spirits and the unconscious mind.

- **Blue Candles**

Blue is incredibly calming and can assist in meditation. It is also healing for the mind and soul. Dark blue is associated with self-expression and art, whereas light blue is associated with dreams and the third eye. Blue is also a masculine color.

- **Red Candles**

Red is the color of blood and reflects our carnal desires. It is visceral, animal, and of the flesh as well as highly energized. Use red candles in rituals related to sex, passion, love, and sensuality.

- **Orange Candles**

Orange candles can be used when dealing with attraction, whether you're trying to attract people, feelings, material goods, or goals. It's also associated with confidence and spirituality.

- **Violet/Fuchsia Candles**

Violet is the color of the divine. If you're trying to connect to a higher place or your higher self, violet candles can invite a more elevated spirituality into your life. Violet is also royal and can assist in enhancing your power and authority.

- **Pink Candles**

Whereas red is sexual, pink deals with romantic love. Pink candles can be helpful in rituals dealing with committed relationships, seeking stability, or elevating the passion between partners. It can also help you tap into feminine energies and is associated with new birth.

- **Brown Candles**

Brown candles help connect us to the earth. It is natural and material, and because of its association with waste or impurities, it can be helpful when attempting to purify something physically or spiritually.

- **Gold Candles**

Gold calls upon the energy of the sun and spirits associated with it. Gold is also associated with money, wealth, and abundance.

- **Grey Candles**

Grey candles can be used similarly to silver candles to call upon feminine or lunar energy. They can also be used in place of brown candles as a means to purify something. Overall, though, grey is a neutral tone and has a muted, disappearing effect.

*Common Hoodoo Candles*

If you're looking for a candle for a very specific purpose or spell, you can buy candles from Hoodoo or witchcraft stores that have been crafted for specific purposes. Make sure you're working with a reputable dealer. This will also give you an idea of how to focus your own candle-making in the future.

- **Adam and Eve**

This candle will help increase your sexual desire and attractiveness and can be used to strengthen a marriage.

- **Adam and Steve**

These candles, which usually smell heavily of patchouli, are used to strengthen the relationship between two men, romantic or otherwise.

- **Alice and Eve**

Alice and Eve candles are used to strengthen the relationship and partnership between two women.

- **Come to Me**

Use this candle to make yourself more attractive to the person you want.

- **Court Case**

Use this candle to assist you in legal battles.

- **Seven Day**

A seven-day candle is a tall cylindrical candle with seven wax discs, one for each day of the week, and is called upon specifically in some week-long spells.

- **Spiritual Cleansing**

Spiritual cleansing candles often include sage and are used to clear negative thoughts, energies, spirits, and feelings to facilitate a positive environment for your work.

- **Road Opener**

Use this candle to clear obstacles from your path. This is great if you're traveling or going on a new journey.

- **Lucky 7**

These candles are sweet and spicy and will help increase your luck and fortune. Use this if you're trying to win a gamble or at a game.

- **Money Draw**

As the title implies, this candle will help you bring more wealth into your life.

- **Reversing**

These are sometimes referred to as "return to sender" candles. If you feel someone is attacking or cursing you, you can use this candle in your rituals to send the effects of their work back at them. You can enhance this ritual by setting the candle on top of a picture of the person you know is attacking you.

- **Steady Job**

This candle will help you find and maintain steady employment and income. Use this if you're looking to increase your financial stability.

- **Tranquil Home**

Use this to deal with fighting, arguments, and malcontent in your household. You can also use a Tranquil Home candle to bless a new home.

- **Uncrossing**

This powerful candle will help you remove curses, spells, negative energy, and anything spiritual that might be causing you harm.

- **Crown of Glory**

This candle will help you succeed and attract prosperity.

- **Double Action**

Double Action candles include two colors and are meant to repel the bad and attract the good. For example, a black and red candle will help you repel whatever is stopping you from finding romantic bliss and attracting your beloved.

- **Stop Gossip**

Use this candle to stop the spread of harmful stories and fix their negative effects. You can enhance the results of this candle by inscribing the name of the gossip or burning the candle on top of their picture.

- **High John the Conqueror**

High John the Conqueror root is incredibly powerful. This candle will help you fight your battles and overcome obstacles.

- **Jinx Remover**

Use this candle to remove curses, confusion, pain, or any force of evil in your life.

## *How to Make Your Own Candle*

There are many benefits to making your own candles. Through the process of making your candle with your own hands, you can infuse your energies and intentions. You can also do this by making natural herb dyes for your candles, though if you do this, make sure to be incredibly purposeful with what herbs and colors you utilize and consider what you plan to use your candle for.

- **Oil Candles**

Oil candles are cheap and easy to make, and you can easily dye the oil. You'll first need an old glass bottle, such as a wine or vinegar bottle, that's been cleaned, had the labels removed, and has been consecrated. You'll also need a cotton wick, a funnel, bottle stoppers, and lamp oil. There are several different types of lamp oil. Remember, the more natural, the better, so seek out olive, fish, castor, canola, or palm kernel oil and avoid kerosene.

*Step One*: Use the funnel to fill up your bottle with oil. Different oils burn at different rates, but generally, two grams of oil will burn for 12 hours.

*Step Two*: Thread your wick through the bottle stopper.

*Step Three*: Place your wick into the bottle so that the bottom touches the oil. Let it soak for 5-10 minutes before you light it.

- **Beeswax Candle**

You'll need the following ingredients: a sheet of beeswax, a cotton candle wick, and a knife (100% beeswax candles tend to burn for 100 hours per 1 lb. for pillar candles, so keep that in mind.)

*Step One*: Cut a square out of the sheet of beeswax.

*Step Two*: Fold the square of beeswax without breaking it.

*Step Three*: Cut a piece of the wick that's just a little bit longer than the wax square. Lay the wick in the fold of the wax so a bit sticks out at the end.

*Step Four*: Start gently rolling the candle into a tube shape. Make sure the wick is firmly in the middle.

*Step Five*: Once you've molded the candle, use your thumbs to mold the bottom of the candle together and close it around the wick.

- **Two-Tone Multi-Wick Candle**

This candle requires exact measurements, but feel free to scale up or down for the particular container you're going to put your candle in. You'll need the following ingredients: 450 grams of paraffin wax, 50 grams of stearin powder, a protractor, a ruler, a sheet of paper, scissors, a needle, 25 cm of a 4-cm-wide wick, a knife, a spoon, greaseproof paper,

15-cm-diameter heat-resistant glass bowl, two bain-marie pans, and two different colors of dyed flakes.

*Step One*: Draw a circle on your piece of paper with a 14-cm diameter.

*Step Two*: Cut the circle out and find the center. Use your protractor to divide your circle into three equal sections. Measure 3.5 cm from the center of the circle on each line and poke a hole there with your needle. This is where you'll be placing your wicks.

*Step Three*: Heat ¾ of your wax in the bain-marie pot to 82 degrees Celsius or 179 degrees Fahrenheit.

*Step Four*: Dip your wick into the melted wax to coat it and set it aside.

*Step Five*: In your other bain-marie pot, heat ¾ of your stearin to 82 degrees Celsius or 179 Fahrenheit.

*Step Six*: Stir your first dye color into the stearin.

*Step Seven*: Pour your dyed stearin into the wax and stir. Test the color by putting a few drops onto your greaseproof paper and letting it dry.

*Step Eight*: Pour your dyed wax into the glass container up to 3 cm. Store or discard the rest and clean out your bain-marie pots.

*Step Nine*: Allow your wax to cool until it's rubbery to the touch, about 75 minutes.

*Step Ten*: Heat your remaining wax in one bain-marie pot and your remaining stearin in the other.

*Step Eleven*: Add your second dye color into the stearin and stir the mixture into your wax.

*Step Twelve*: Pour your wax over the first layer of wax up to about 1.2 cm. Store or discard the rest.

*Step Thirteen*: Let the top layer of the wax set until rubbery. Lay your piece of paper on top of the wax and use your needle to poke the holes you made into the wax. Discard the paper and poke the hole all the way down into the wax.

*Step Fourteen*: Cut 3 pieces of equal length coated wick and insert them into your candle. Cut them about 1.5 cm from the top of the wax.

*Step Fifteen*: Let the candle sit until cool, then take it out of the glass bowl.

### When to Burn Your Candles

Being conscious about when you're doing candle magic and how that magic is interacting with the cycles of the sun and moon can help enhance your spells and rituals.

**Lunar Cycles**

- **New Moon**

The new moon is associated with purification rituals and will amplify the effects of your spell.

- **Full Moon**

The full moon is associated with maturation and is a good time to focus on rituals about oneself.

- **Crescent Moon**

If you have goals that need to be completed urgently, do them during the crescent moon.

- **Waning Moon**

The waning moon is associated with solving health issues, overcoming obstacles, and resolving gossip. You'll also get long-lasting results from these rituals.

**Days of the Week**

- **Monday: Day of the Moon**

Colors: light blue, pastel green, and white

Oils/incense: jasmine, ginger, and sandalwood

- **Tuesday: Day of Mars**

Colors: bordeaux and red

Oils/Incense: hot pepper, black pepper, geranium, and nettle

- **Wednesday: Day of Mercury**

Colors: dark green, beige, copper, and light yellow

Oils/incense: cumin, fennel, cinnamon, lavender, and chamomile

- **Thursday: Day of Jupiter**

Colors: violet, turquoise, and blue

Oils/incense: mint, cedar, nutmeg, benzoin, and saffron

- **Friday**

Colors: pink and green

Oils/incense: rose, myrtle, orange blossom, and apple

- **Saturday**

Colors: black, olive green, and dark brown

Oils/incense: musk, cypress, dandelion, and myrrh

- **Sunday**

Colors: orange, silver, yellow, and gold

Oils/incense: laurel, saffron, cinnamon, olibanum, and orange

### Candle Spells and Rituals

If you are doing candle magic, you'll first need to consecrate your candle. You can do this using a holy oil that you've either bought or that you have made yourself, as we will discuss later on. Hold your candle in your left hand and dip the fingers on your right hand into the oil. If the goal of your ritual is to attract, rub the candle from wick to base with the base facing toward you. If your goal is to repel or ward something off, move from base to wick, still with the base facing toward you. This is also the point where you might engrave your intentions.

For a basic candle spell, hold your candle to your head and meditate on your intentions. You can use tealight candles or incense to assist in this. After some time, once you feel you have fully imbued your intentions, place your candle in its stand and light it. Cup your hands around the flame and, while you encounter the heart of the flame, further your intentions by meditating or reciting prayers, invocations, or verses. The exact words you use are up to you and your relationship to the spiritual. Again, you must trust your intuition. Once you feel the ritual is complete, simply let the candle burn out. However, you don't want to leave the room or ignore your candle now that you have closed the ritual, as there is important information that could be communicated to you.

### ▸ Candle Divination

Even if the candle is not the focus of the ritual, the way candles behave during your spiritual practices can be examined and used for divination. Avoiding strange drafts or moving air in your altar space will help to make sure you're not getting mixed messages or disrupting the burning process.

- **Flame Jumps**

This signals struggles and the presence of opposition.

- **Flame Burns Very High**

This is a good sign. Your spiritual work is progressing quickly, and the spirits or deities you are working with are doing what you need.

- **Flame Burns Very Low**

The meaning of a low flame depends on what kind of spell you're doing. If you're working towards protection or prosperity, you might need to cleanse your environment, as negative energy is interfering in your spellcasting. It may also mean you have problems that need to be addressed before you can access the power of the spirits towards this goal.

If your spell is an offensive one, a curse, or an attack on another person, this means that your adversary is incredibly powerful and protected, and you need to take further steps or employ other rituals to achieve your desired goal.

- **White Smoke**

You will get what you have asked for in your ritual, but not without some struggle.

- **Lots of Black Smoke**

Negative energies and forces are interfering with your work. You should cleanse the area and yourself of negative energy. If you're attempting an attack or curse, you should stop the ritual, as you risk that negativity coming back to you and causing harm.

- **Lots of Black Smoke Only in the Beginning**

This also symbolizes the need for cleansing, but, in this case, the candle is burning some of that. There have been difficulties achieving your goal, but you may still achieve it.

- **Candle Catches Fire**

This indicates that something should have been done before the ritual began and that these things will cause difficulty in achieving your goal. This could be a spiritual issue, such as failing to cleanse or communicate with the spirits of your ancestors. It could also be something in your life. If you're launching an attack or curse, your adversary has already detected that you are trying to harm them and has taken action.

- **Candle Burns Unevenly or Partially**

This indicates that you probably did something incorrectly in your ritual, or you are using the wrong tools or rituals to achieve your specific goal. You will get what you want but only partially.

- **Multiple Flames**

Multiple flames indicate multiple forces, with the main one being you. If your goal is love, the other flames may represent rivals or outside forces that might come between you and your beloved. If the goal is protection, it represents multiple adversaries. If the goal is an attack, it represents the allies of your adversary.

- **Flickering**

Flickering is the candle struggling to stay lit. This indicates that there are spirits present and that your spiritual power may be insufficient. If your goal is protection, you aren't yet spiritually powerful enough for the spell you're attempting, and you should fix that through cleansing or a ritual bath for protection. If your goal is to attract something like love or wealth, there are spiritual obstacles that are keeping you from being as powerful as you need to be. If your goal is an attack, your adversary has already foiled your attempts to harm them.

- **Cracking or Popping Noises**

An adversary is working against you. The volume of the pops is equivalent to the power of that enemy.

- **Flame Color**

Flames burn on a color spectrum, with blue being the hottest and red being the coolest. A blue flame means that there is a benevolent spirit present. This can be a helpful deity or an ancestor. Red signifies that a very powerful entity is present. Yellow and orange indicate the presence of helpful energy.

## OILS

Oils hold significance in almost any culture. They are the soul and essence of the thing they are derived from. However, the use of oils in Hoodoo goes beyond simply aromatherapy or natural medicine. Oils help enhance and seal the spiritual power and energy of a thing. They can be used to invoke and consecrate. When you place an oil on that thing, you are imbuing it with the oil's power. You can also use powders made from plants in a similar manner.

You can buy oil blends made specifically for Hoodoo or magical purposes, though make sure to investigate whether or not the seller is trustworthy. You also lose the benefit of the added power that comes with making your oils and imbuing them with your energy. If you're making your own oils, be sure to get essential oils that are pure as opposed to watered-down oils or artificial fragrances. You can use your oil to anoint yourself or objects. You can also put your oil into an amulet or talisman. Make sure to store your oil in a cool, dry place in a dark-colored glass bottle. Use them within six months.

If you're directing a spell towards a specific person, powders and oils can be used to enhance that spell by sprinkling them in a place where that person usually walks. You can seal this intent by speaking their name as you do this. You can use this both to attract and repel. You can also put oil or powder on a candle to enhance the results of candle magic.

*Making Your Own Oils*

The first step to creating your own oil is having a base oil. These are neutral oils that will carry the powerful oils in each recipe. They also dilute the essential oils, which is important as many essential oils can be dangerous when put directly on the skin. The common base oils are almond, coconut, grapeseed, jojoba, safflower, or sunflower. To mix your oil, swirl them clockwise. You'll also need a standard-sized eyedropper. You can use your knowledge of herbs to make your own personalized and specific oils, but here are a few commonly used oil recipes.

- **Abramelin Oil**

This is a ceremonial oil that dates back to the Bible. The different ingredients have specific symbolism. While it differs somewhat from the Judeo-Christian interpretation, in Hoodoo, the olive symbolizes a happy and stable home, myrrh is sacred to God, galanga symbolizes protection, cinnamon symbolizes money, and calamus protects from the evil eye and for good luck.

You'll need: ½ a tablespoon of cinnamon oil, 1 tablespoon of myrrh oil, 1 tablespoon of calamus oil, 1 tablespoon of cassia oil, and 7 tablespoons of olive oil.

*Step One*: Add your essential oils into your olive oil.

*Step Two*: Swirl and store.

- **Altar Oil**

This is a great oil to keep at your altar to bless yourself or your ritual items. You'll need: 4 drops of frankincense oil, 2 drops of myrrh oil, 1 drop of cedar oil, and 2 oz. of olive oil.

*Step One*: Add your essential oils into your olive oil.

*Step Two*: Swirl and store.

- **Attraction Oil**

This will help attract everything positive, including love, money, and prosperity. You'll need: 1 tablespoon of grated lemon peel or lemon flowers, 1 tablespoon of lovage, 2oz. of grapeseed oil, and one small piece of magnetite.

*Step One*: Mix together your lemon peel or flowers and lovage.

*Step Two*: Add your mixture into the grapeseed oil and swirl.

*Step Three*: Place a piece of magnetite into each bottle and store.

- **Anointing Oil**

This is a quick and easy oil recipe that can be used for blessing and consecration. You'll need: 35 drops of frankincense, 35 drops of myrrh, and 1 oz. of olive oil.

*Step One*: Add your essential oils into your olive oil.

*Step Two*: Swirl and store.

- **Quick Van Van Oil**

Van Van Oil is an age-old recipe. It brings good luck, prosperity, wealth and will overall attract positive energies. You'll need the following ingredients: 2 tablespoons of lemongrass herb, 2 drops of lemongrass oil, 2 oz. almond oil, and a small piece of blessed rock salt

*Step One*: Add your lemongrass herb and oils into your almond oil and swirl.

*Step Two*: Add your piece of rock salt and store.

- **Van Van Oil**

You'll need the following ingredients: 8 full droppers of lemongrass oil, 4 full droppers of citronella oil, ½ a dropper of vetiver oil, ½ a dropper of palmarosa oil, ½ a dropper of ginger grass oil, a pinch of dried lemongrass leaves, a pinch of crushed pyrite, and 1 ounce of almond oil.

*Step One*: Mix all of your essential oils, excluding the almond oil, together and let them sit for a week.

*Step Two*: Add the dried lemongrass leaves, crushed pyrite, and almond oil.

*Step Three*: Swirl and store.

- **Come To Me Oil**

This is an attraction oil and will help you bring love and romance into your life by drawing people's eyes. You'll need the following ingredients: 7 drops of cinnamon oil, 6 drops of jasmine oil, 1 drop of ginger oil, ½ dropper of patchouli oil, small pieces of a cinnamon stick, and 1 oz. of grapeseed oil.

*Step One*: Swirl together and store in a colored glass.

- **All Saints Oil**

All Saints oil is said to call upon the Saints to aid you. It brings healing, blessings, and success. You'll need the following ingredients: ½ dropper of cinnamon oil, ½ dropper of rose oil, ½ dropper of gardenia oil, ½ dropper of vetiver oil, ½ teaspoon of patchouli oil, 1 crushed whole vanilla bean, and 1 oz. of almond oil.

*Step One*: Swirl together and store.

- **Crown of Success Oil**

As the name suggests, this oil will help bring your success in any aspect of life and will assist you in overcoming barriers and hurdles in pursuit of your goals. You'll need the following ingredients: ½ teaspoon of Aloes Wood, ½ teaspoon of bay leaf, ½ teaspoon of copal, ½ teaspoon of vetiver, ½ teaspoon of sandalwood, and 1 oz. olive oil

*Step One*: Grind up all of your dry ingredients.

*Step Two*: Add one teaspoon of the mixture into your olive oil.

*Step Three*: Pour this into an amber bottle and leave it to sit in the sunlight for a day.

- **Master Key Oil**

Master Key oil will grant you power over any situation, problem, or spell. It will allow you to unlock your mind and soul to access your deepest desires and your true powers. You'll need the following ingredients: ¼ teaspoon of Master Root, ¼ teaspoon of cinnamon, ¼ teaspoon of frankincense, ¼ teaspoon of galangal root, ¼ teaspoon of myrrh, ¼ teaspoon of patchouli, ¼ teaspoon of sage, ¼ teaspoon of star anise, ¼ teaspoon of vervain, ¼ teaspoon of crushed vanilla bean, 1 small key, and 2 oz. of almond oil.

*Step One*: Mix all of your herbs together.

*Step Two*: Add one teaspoon of this mixture into your almond oil.

*Step Three*: Pour this mixture into an amber bottle.

*Step Four*: Place the key inside of the oil and store it.

- **Confusion Oil**

Use this oil to disrupt the minds of your adversaries and bring chaos and confusion into any situation that you wish to have an advantage over. You'll need the following ingredients: 1 full dropper of vetiver oil, 1 full dropper of marjoram oil, 2 full droppers of patchouli oil, 2 teaspoons of grains of paradise, 2 teaspoons of poppy seeds, 2 teaspoons of black mustard seed, and 2 oz. of grapeseed oil.

*Step One*: Mix together your dry herbs and essential oil, excluding the grapeseed oil.

*Step Two*: Add 2 tablespoons of the mixture to your grapeseed oil.

*Step Three*: Swirl and store.

- **Uncrossing Oil**

Uncrossing oil removes negative energies and can help you disconnect yourself from negative forces. It can help reflect negative energy that's been sent towards you back to its source. You'll need the following ingredients: 3 drops of vetiver, 2 drops of clove oil, 1 drop of cedarwood oil, and 2 oz. of almond oil.

*Step One*: Mix your essential oils together, excluding the almond oil.

*Step Two*: Add two tablespoons of this mixture into the almond oil.

*Step Three*: Swirl and store.

- **Fast Luck Oil**

Use this to increase your luck in any aspect of your life. You'll need the following ingredients: 2 drops of dragon's blood oil, 2 drops of lemon oil, 2 drops of rosemary oil, 1 drop of cinnamon oil, and 1 oz. of sunflower oil.

*Step One*: Add your sunflower oil into a dark glass container.

*Step Two*: Swirl in your essential oils and store.

## BONES

Bones are a common divination tool across magical practices. They are a tool to communicate with one's deities and ancestors and glean spiritual knowledge they wouldn't have otherwise been able to know. Therefore, in order to start doing bone divination, you need to make sure you have an active relationship with your ancestors and that you are mentally and spiritually cleansed and clear.

In bone divination, every bone has a specific, set meaning. The bones are thrown on the ground or on a marked cloth, and the position of the specific bones reveals truths. These are, of course, animal bones, since despite the media depiction, Hoodoo has no interest in graverobbing and especially no interest in disrespecting the corpses of our ancestors. You can buy bone sets specifically for divination. You can also go out into nature and collect animal bones and use those primarily or add them to a pre-bought set. Your bone collection can also include things like charms, dice, stones, keys, etc.

Keep in mind that bone divination is also a difficult practice, one that will take not only constant trial and error but acute intuition and listening to the messages of your deities and ancestors. For this reason, every bone reader has their own style and method. Seek out other bone readers and take advantage of the wisdom of those who are more experienced than you.

### Preparing for Divination

You'll first need to bless and consecrate each bone with oil, holy liquid, and/or incense. Then, take each item of your set and, at your altar, present it to your ancestors and tell them what that piece means. By doing this, you're establishing a shared language that will allow your ancestors to communicate with you. When you're not using your bones, store them safely and respectfully at your altar.

### *Different Reading Surfaces*

Once you've established your bone set to your ancestors, you'll need to pick what kind of reading surface you're going to be using. This is the cloth or material that you'll be consistently throwing your bones on. Regardless of what you choose, you'll need to practice a few times to get a feel for how to throw the bones so that they spread out and nothing gets broken. Once again, take the time to find your rhythm and trust your intuition and spiritual messages.

- **Designed Mats**

These bone reading mats will have sections marked off to represent different concepts and different aspects of life that you can then use to interpret your bones. For example, a mat might have sections for business, family, health, etc. There are also many mats that use the zodiac. You can also design your own mat with designated sections, as long as you are sure as to what each section means beforehand.

- **Animal Pelts**

Another common reading surface is an animal pelt, sometimes from the same species as the bone set. In this case, the bone reading is interpreted based on what body part of the animal the bones fall on.

*Head*

This indicates the person's current mental state, thoughts, and questions regarding the bones.

*Neck*

The neck represents external forces in the person's life.

*Chest*

Bones falling on the chest indicate something about the person's feelings, desires, and true motivations.

*Left Front Paw*

This represents opposition against the person seeking divination.

*Left Hind Leg*

This represents past events and historical influences.

*Right Front Paw*

Bones falling here address the 'correct' path and the things the person needs to do in order to address their situation, as well as the friends and allies they have.

*Right Hind Leg*

This represents the future of the current situation.

*Groin*

The groin deals with sex, sexuality, and consistent patterns of thoughts and actions, both negative and positive.

*Tail/Anus*

Bones falling here represent the lessons the person needs to learn from the situation.

**How to Read the Bones**

A divination ritual starts with a core question. Once the question has been asked, the bones are tossed on the mat. The first major factor in reading the bones is orientation. Similar to Tarot, it's up to the reader which way they want to orient the bones. In a left/right orientation reading, the bones are read as being on a timeline from left to right, with the left being the past and the right being the future. You can also read this as the bones that are closest to the reader being the past and the ones further away being the future. You can also read bones without a linear timeline.

With all the specifics of your bone divination decided, it will still take time before you should feel comfortable offering divination to anyone else. Start by telling your own fortune at your altar. Each morning, pull one bone from your bag and assess its predetermined meaning. See that as your daily fortune. As you get more and more comfortable with bone reading, try taking out a handful of bones and scattering them on your altar. Keep a journal of all of your readings and keep communication with the spirits open so you can monitor your own growth and comfort with bone reading.

## CONCLUSION

While other Hoodoo tools are used to facilitate magic and create a space where it is possible, candles, oils, and bones will help you bring power to your work. By understanding these essential magical items, you will better be able to communicate with spirits, focus your mind and intentions, and seek out your goals.

# 7

# MOJO BAGS AND SWEETENING JARS

While candles and oils are items that are used for various magical purposes, you can also imbue physical items with magical properties for a specific purpose. We will discuss two of the most common magical items: mojo or conjure bags and sweetening jars.

## WHAT MAKES A MOJO BAG

Mojo bags are another commonly misunderstood and misrepresented aspect of Hoodoo. In fact, mojo bags are the culmination of many different Hoodoo practices and are the most personal items in a Hoodoo practitioner's life.

A mojo bag is a sort of talisman or charm, a physical item that is worn or carried that holds spiritual and magical significance. They are tied to your soul, your destiny, your dreams, your desires and cannot be used by anyone else. Whereas spells are single-minded requests that are asked for and then fulfilled, a mojo bag is a constant magical force. Their work is never done, unlike a spell.

Mojo bags are thus extremely potent, and mishandling them or dealing with them lightly could cause harm. You risk amplifying negative forces or energies in your life if you aren't careful and purposeful with the creation of your mojo bag. However, with this high risk is a high reward.

Mojo bags are living, dynamic things that need to be treated with love, respect, and dignity. Just as our physical bodies are conduits for the spiritual, the mojo bag is the physical body through which the magical work will be done. Like human bodies, while each mojo bag has similar components, they are also entirely unique.

### The Body

Mojo bags are made of some sort of cloth that is stuffed with at least one spiritual or magical item. They are then sealed with a drawstring. While they're commonly made with red flannel, especially in the South, they can also be made of leather or suede and can abide by magical color theory to enhance their purpose.

The magical items placed inside the mojo bag are incredibly personal to the practitioner. Herbs, stones, charms, oils, bark, prayers written on paper, almost anything can be included in your mojo bag as long as they are meaningful within your practice. When you collect these items and put them in your mojo bag, the individual spirits come together to create one spiritual force that works on your behalf.

Some people sell mojo bags as being double or triple strength. This means that they include items that are either extremely rare or difficult to create, or they include more items than normal.

### *A Name*

You can choose your name based on spiritual intuition. For example, if you have a dream about a certain name or if you keep finding yourself drawn to and thinking about a specific name. You can also choose to name your mojo bag after a figure who represents what you want to achieve with your mojo bag. If you're an artist seeking great success and notoriety, you could name your bag "Picasso" or "Vermeer." You can also draw upon religious symbols like saints or spirits. Once your bag has a name, you can use that name whenever you interact with your mojo bag.

### *Caring for Your Mojo Bag*

Since your mojo bag is alive, it needs to be treated with love, respect, and care. Firstly, a mojo bag is usually created at your altar space, so make sure to cleanse and purify the area beforehand. After you initially make your mojo bag, you'll want to wear it on your person, under your clothes, and below your waist for at least a week, though you can continue past that. Also, make sure to sleep with it close by.

You must feed your mojo bag once a week on the same day it was created every week. You can do this with oils, alcohol, and even bodily fluids depending on the purpose and your relationship with your mojo bag.

Mojo bags should also be kept private. No one other than you should see or touch your mojo bag. When wearing it, secure it under your clothes. Someone else seeing or touching your mojo bag can result in it losing its power. If this happens, give your mojo bag water from a Rose of Jericho, as it is a resurrection plant. Pray over your mojo bag and, if you feel it is still alive and working, continue to protect it. If, however, your mojo bag is dead, it should be buried properly.

Mojo bags generally live for about a year, but there's no need to replace it if it continues to work for you after this time. If your mojo bag starts to wear down, disassemble it and keep the hard items like rocks or charms while discarding things like herbs. Reassemble the mojo bag and give it new life with a prayer and a feeding of incense smoke.

## BASIC MOJO BAGS

When making your mojo bag, your spiritual and magical intuition trumps any formal recipe. This isn't a one-size-fits-all charm. It is just as personal to you as a child. However, it can be helpful to have some examples of what a mojo bag made for different purposes might look like, and a recipe can be a great starting place for creating yours. Each bag should be assembled by first placing all of the charms inside, smoking your bag with a related incense, reciting a prayer or chant, and finally feeding the bag with oil.

- **Money**

You'll need: a red or green flannel bag, a coin, 1 buckeye, five finger grass, silverweed, clove, cinnamon, a pair of lodestones, Money Drawing Oil, and money drawing incense.

- **Come To Me**

You'll need: a pink or red bag, a physical piece of yourself and the person you want to attract, such as hair or fingernails, a pair of lodestones, a seal of Venus pendant, dirt from a church or wedding chapel, lovage root, tonka bean, Spanish saffron, damiana leaf, violet, catnip, roses, coriander seed, licorice root, gentian root, spikenard, lavender, passionflower, sugar, three ming's incense, and Love Me Oil.

- **Good Health**

You'll need: a red or green flannel bag, a piece of yourself such as hair or fingernails, rose petals, rosemary, eucalyptus, cayenne, health oil, and health incense.

- **Business**

You'll need: a green bag, dirt from a successful local business or bank, cinnamon chips, Irish moss, alkanet root, St. Joseph beans, a piece of pyrite, a lodestone, money, your business card, three kings incense, and Better Business Oil.

- **Peace**

You'll need: a blue or indigo flannel bag, a seashell, lapis lazuli, chamomile, and a symbol of peace.

MAJOR USES FOR A MOJO BAG

While the use of a mojo bag comes in its specific construction, they fall under three major categories of intent.

*Attract Your Desires*

If you have a large, lifelong goal or a deep burning desire for something that can't be achieved through simple, individual spells, you can use a mojo bag to draw that thing toward you as you move through daily life. This is a much better alternative than completing the same spell over and over again every week, as you can dedicate your mojo bag to that particular spell and have it working at all times.

### *Enhance Protection*

One of the major historical uses for mojo bags was as protection for travelers, especially if they were entering unknown territory. A mojo bag can help to enhance a protection spell you've already cast and surround you with a barrier against negative forces and spiritual attacks. It can even reflect negative energies or curses sent toward you back to their source.

### *Enhance Your Inner Strength*

Every person has a deep well of immense power within them. For many reasons, we lose connection to this power. Through being disconnected from our history, our ancestors, or knowledge about the spiritual realm, we can lose awareness of our true abilities. Mojo bags can help you tap into your power and bring it forth to utilize in your life. Being aware and entrenched in this power can help bring you peace and confidence in even the most trying of circumstances.

## SWEETENING JARS

Sweetening jars are oftentimes the first magic act new Hoodoo practitioners create. As the name suggests, they exist to 'sweeten' something or someone to you. They can be used to make people kinder, more willing, or more gracious to you. They can be used to strengthen relationships, whether the goal is to reconcile with a distant loved one or encourage your boss to give you a raise. These are popular items because they are relatively easy to make, and one jar can be used for months at a time.

### Basic Construction of a Sweetening Jar

The first thing you need is a glass jar with a metal lid. The metal lid is a necessity, as you'll be burning a candle on top of it. You can use a particular colored candle that corresponds with your desires, though a tea light or white candle will also work perfectly as you'll be filling your jar with magical items.

Inside your jar, you'll need a base sweetening liquid. This could be sugar, maple syrup, honey, or Karo. After that, you'll then need to add an odd number of magical items related to your goals, including herbs, taglocks, and stones. You'll also need to use petition papers, also known as prayer papers.

Once you get what you want out of your jar, bury it with respect.

### ▸ How To Make Petition Papers

Petition papers are a way to express your prayers and desires. During slavery, paper was incredibly hard to come by, so many Hoodoo practitioners would use scraps of the brown paper bags they received their rations in. Some modern practitioners follow in that tradition and use brown paper bags for their papers, though there are many ways to be expressive with your papers. You can use colored paper or documents related to your desire. You can also express your desires through the color ink that you use.

For the purpose of sweetening jars, you'll be writing both your name and the person you want to target's name on separate pieces of paper an odd number of times. Writing a name three times is neutral. Seven times is related to attraction and good luck and can help bring long-term change. Writing a name nine times asserts dominance and control as it is incredibly powerful. Thirteen is a very superstitious number and is used in offense against one's enemies. You can also write a name backward in order to send something or someone away from you.

After you write these names, write the following words in a circle around the name without lifting up your pen: opppurtunityworkrewardsoppurtunityworkrewards… Again, make sure you do not lift the pen until the circle is complete or you'll need to start over.

Anoint your papers with oils and/or powders. Place appropriate charms or herbs on your paper. Say your desires outside, then fold the paper toward you in half. Turn the paper and fold it toward you again, then repeat a third time. Eat a dollop of honey and repeat your desires.

- **Honey Jar for Career Prosperity**

You'll need: honey, petition papers, your own taglocks, a taglock of your boss or manager if possible, a lodestone, magnetic sand, High John the Conqueror Oil, dirt from a place related to your career goals, a glass jar, and a green candle.

You'll also need an odd number of any combination of the following herbs: cinnamon, five finger grass, galangal, patchouli, chamomile, grains of paradise, devil's shoestring, and gravel root.

*Step One*: Add everything except your candle into your jar.

*Step Two*: Seal tightly.

*Step Three*: Place your green candle on the lid and burn for seven straight days.

*Step Four*: Burn the candle three days a week until you get the job.

- **Honey Jar for Love**

You'll need: honey, petition papers, your own taglocks, a taglock of your beloved, a lodestone representing you, a glass jar, a lodestone representing your beloved, Desire Me Oil, Come to Me Oil, and a pink or red candle.

You'll also need an odd number of any combination of the following herbs: lovage, gardenia, violet, cubeb berries, tonka beans, coriander, rosebuds, vanilla, ginger, balm of gilead, lavender, damiana, catnip, and deer's tongue leaf.

*Step One*: Add everything except your candle into your jar.

*Step Two*: Seal tightly.

*Step Three*: Place your pink or red candle on the lid and burn for seven straight days.

*Step Four*: Burn the candle three days a week until you have the desired results.

- **Honey Jar for Money**

You'll need: honey, pyrite stone, lodestone, a mercury dime, a glass jar, your own taglock, Money Drawing Oil, money-drawing powder, and a green or white candle.

You'll also need an odd number of any combination of the following herbs: cinnamon sticks, allspice, sage, cedar, clove, galangal, peppermint, basil, and pine.

*Step One*: Add everything except your candle into your jar.

*Step Two*: Seal tightly.

*Step Three*: Shake your jar, then place your green candle on the lid and let it melt completely.

*Step Four*: Repeat this daily. Keep a small votive or tealight burning on your jar to enhance the spell.

## CONCLUSION

Mojo bags and honey jars are great ways to utilize our spiritual power in a way that doesn't require constant spellcasting. These are important tools for helping you maintain the presence of magic in your life. Mojo bags require dignity and respect, and in exchange, they will be a constant and powerful ally at all times. Sweetening jars, on the other hand, can help you tackle any problem, hurdle, or relationship in your life by making anything just a little bit sweeter.

# AFTERWORD

Like black culture, Hoodoo is the combination of countless different cultures and religions, many of which are untraceable and have been lost to time, violence, and oppression. This combination has resulted in an impossible harmony that is reflective of the black spirit. The immense creativity, willpower, wit, compassion, and love that has allowed black people to continue to live and create is what fuels Hoodoo.

How you practice could look completely different from the work of another practitioner. The prayers you say, the tools you use, the spirits and entities you work with, and how you work with them, the extent to which Hoodoo influences your life and social circles, all of this depends on the unique circumstances of your life. What is most important is following the core concepts of Hoodoo in a way that makes sense to you.

Hoodoo is about using the physical world around you to influence the spiritual. To do that, you must connect with the Earth through understanding and interacting with plants, soil, and natural elements which all contain a unique and potent spirit. By understanding and respecting these natural spirits, you can influence the world around you to your own will.

Hoodoo allows you to defend yourself and even cause harm, if it is necessary, in the search for noble vengeance. However, Hoodoo is not about hoarding power over others. It is about bringing about more happiness for yourself and the ones you love and tapping into the spiritual realm. The spiritual forces we as Hoodoo practitioners use are far out of our human comprehension, and they are not to be dealt with flippantly; attempting to abuse these forces or treating them without respect could lead to dire consequences.

It would be impossible to explain the depth and breadth of Hoodoo in an entire lifetime, let alone in one book. I hope that this is the first step on a very long journey of discovering the spiritual and connecting with the world through this beautiful practice. If this book has led you to make your life and the lives of people around you better, please leave a review so that others might be led down the same path.

## LEAVE A 1-CLICK REVIEW

If you enjoyed this book, it would be incredibly helpful if you could take a few moments to write a brief review on Amazon, even if it's just a few sentences!
Below is a QR code that will take you to the page where you can leave your review.

**Thanks in advance!**

# REFERENCES

*About hoodoo witchcraft.* HoodooWitch. (n.d.). https://www.hoodoowitch.net/about-hoodoo-witch/

Belard, A. (2020). *Hoodoo for beginners: Working magic spells in rootwork and conjure with roots, herbs, candles, and oils.* Hentopan Publishing.

Elias, S. (2019, March 2). *How to build an ancestor altar. Crescent city conjure.* https://crescentcityconjure.us/blogs/city-of-conjure/how-to-build-an-ancestor-altar

Lane, M. (2008). *Hoodoo heritage: A brief history of american folk religion.* Appalachian State University.

Moorehouse-Rutgers, E. D. (2013, January 4). *African-American Hoodoo: more than magic.* Futurity. https://www.futurity.org/african-american-hoodoo-more-than-magic/

Nittle, N. (2020, October 30). *'We're reclaiming these traditions': black women embrace the spiritual realm*. NBCNews.com. https://www.nbcnews.com/news/nbcblk/we-re-reclaiming-these-traditions-black-women-embrace-spiritual-realm-n1245488

Wikimedia Foundation. (2021, November 26). *Hoodoo (spirituality)*. Wikipedia. https://en.wikipedia.org/wiki/Hoodoo_(spirituality)

Williamson, M. & Niarè. M. (2021). *HOODOO: 4 books in 1 hoodoo for beginners + spell book + herbal magic + candle magic | a complete introductory guide to traditional folk magic*. Kindle Edition

Siedlak, M. (2018). *Hoodoo: African spirituality beliefs and practices book 1 (2nd Ed)*. Oshun Publications LLC. www.oshunpublications.com

www.ingramcontent.com/pod-product-compliance
Lightning Source LLC
Chambersburg PA
CBHW012004090526
44590CB00026B/3875